You Can't
Fall Off
the Floor...

You Can't Fall Off the Floor...

and
Other Lessons from a
Life in Hollywood

by

Harris Katleman and
Nick Katleman

Rosetta
Books®

To Bess and Michael Katleman, who started it all.
And to my three children, seven grandchildren,
and nine great grandchildren (and counting).
You are my true inspiration and have
filled my life with love.

Table of Contents

Foreword

As a kid, I remember people talking about how Harris Katleman was an iconic figure in entertainment. To me, he was just my grandfather. The only evidence of his career was the Emmy perched on his bar, the picture of him with Grace Kelly in the dining room, and the Simpsons pinball machine in his office. But none of these items seemed to define him—in my eyes, he was a charismatic patriarch with an undeniable presence in the room. It wasn't until I graduated college and started working in the mailroom at WME, a major Hollywood agency, that I recognized my grandfather's stature in the business. Eager to take full advantage of my tenure in entertainment graduate school, I started spending more time with him, if only to hear stories about his escapades in the business. I didn't expect to stumble upon a treasure trove of industry wisdom. Not only did my grandfather have a scholar's grasp on the history of Hollywood, he had savvy insight into the modern trends and active players in the game. I witnessed a new side of him—a side that explained how he had risen to such heights throughout his illustrious career.

As I embarked on a journey to co-write his life experiences, I learned a tremendous amount about the mechanics of the business. But my favorite part of the collaboration was observing my grandfather's raw passion. This is a man who lives and breathes entertainment in the best way possible. We can only hope that his love and enthusiasm for quality programming endures throughout generations to come.

—NICK KATLEMAN

Preface

For the past several decades, I've held two family dinners at my house every year: one for Passover and one for the December holidays. I've had some bright moments over the course of my career, but I don't know a greater joy than sitting with my family together at the dinner table. At some point during every meal, my grandchildren turn to me with lights in their eyes and ask a flurry of questions about my career in the entertainment business.

"How did you get your start in Hollywood?"

"How many famous people do you know?"

"Did you really run Fox Television?"

For years, I dodged their questions, not wanting to bore anyone with stories of a bygone career. But these questions caused me to reflect on my experiences representing talent at MCA, developing shows at Goodson Todman Productions, building a television slate at a production company of my own, and serving as president and chairman of the board at MGM and Twentieth Century Fox. The lessons I've learned not only reflect Hollywood during the dawn of television, they apply to the industry as it stands today. They're also pretty damn entertaining. So I resolved to craft a book not only for my family, but for the future generations of the industry that I love so dearly. I hope that my brightest moments and greatest pitfalls can offer guidance to the rainmakers of tomorrow who are carving their own paths through the business.

As I sat down with my grandson to pen the morsels of wisdom I've acquired, my mind trailed off to the gravelly voice of Marvin Davis, the billionaire oilman who owned Twentieth Century Fox.

"Harris," he told me, "if the Soviets drop a nuke, I want to be standing next to you. You're the consummate survivor."

I'm not sure that I'd make the best doomsday companion, but as I reflect upon the figures with whom I've interacted over the last sixty-five years, I must admit that my career's been colorful. I've played ball with the titans of show business: Lew Wasserman, Jules Stein, Mark Goodson, Kirk Kerkorian, Barry Diller, Marvin Davis, Rupert Murdoch, and all the brightest stars of the mid-twentieth century. I've dedicated my vocation to sculpting narratives for consumption—artificial narratives that thwart the pull of everyday life. And still, the best stories I've experienced have been capped behind screens—in the boardrooms, offices, and restaurants of a desert town called Hollywood.

—HARRIS KATLEMAN

Stars, Scrotums & Mail Carts
1949-1951

On a mild December evening in 1951, I left my office at MCA, the juggernaut of all Hollywood agencies, with plans to grab a cocktail with an industry executive. I was twenty-three years old, living in the heart of the entertainment industry, and cutting my teeth to make a name for myself. Strolling down the palm-lined drive toward the parking lot—ironically the site of today's police station—I noticed a woman with eyes like saucers. She hid behind the steering wheel of her Cadillac watching two men embroiled in a fiery exchange. I turned to find the silhouette of one figure reaching into his jacket pocket. Then, two flashes and two pops sent me leaping behind a signpost. The woman in the Cadillac skidded toward Santa Monica Boulevard as the victim wobbled like a speared bull.

By the time I trotted up to the wounded man, he was curled on the ground with a veil of hate across his face. I was aghast to identify him as Jennings Lang, one of the major executives at the agency.

"... Jennings? Where'd he tag you?!" I asked.

"That two-bit producer blew my balls off!"

As Jennings and I hobbled to my car with the crotch of his suit pants soaked in blood, I found myself whirled into the familiar disorientation that only Hollywood can offer—the same feeling that forced me to ask myself countless times throughout my career, "Where the hell am I?"

I had always thought of Jennings Lang as quick to smile, with a blockish set of teeth polished between thin, sealed lips. Among the major list of names on his client roster, Jennings represented Joan Bennett, who had performed in a number of significant films like *Scarlet Street* and *The*

Woman in the Window. They shared a good relationship that grew a bit too good for Jennings's sake. Though Jennings was a bachelor, Joan had married the German Jewish producer Walter Wanger, who was responsible for classic films like *Arabian Nights* and *Joan of Arc*. Wanger was a rainmaker with relationships at every studio and a European narcissism to match.

Jennings shouldn't have dipped his pen in the ink he was writing with, but he wasn't one for rules. So he commissioned help from his underling Jay Kanter, who rented an unassuming apartment in Beverly Hills just a few blocks from the MCA complex. With a copy of the key, Jennings used the unit to enjoy many an afternoon's delight with his favorite client. A few months in, however, Wanger followed the couple to Jay's apartment, where he confirmed his suspicions of adultery. With a vendetta against Jennings, he stalked the MCA parking lot, waiting to blast my colleague's member to bits.

And thus, I found myself tasked to save Jennings Lang and his overactive testicles. He had taken one bullet in the groin and another in his upper right thigh. My mind immediately sparked to the prospect of getting him to Cedars-Sinai, the best hospital in town. But that wasn't an option. This incident involved some very public figures and had to be managed with discretion. No one wanted this story running in the trades the following morning.

Then it occurred to me: my uncle Phil was chief of staff at Midway Hospital in the Pico-Robertson neighborhood. The medical center was perfect: unassuming and populated by someone I could trust. Now came the issue of transport—I drove a Ford convertible, and though it wasn't a luxurious vehicle, it had a beautiful saddle interior. Tanned leather doesn't fare well with blood splotches. I laid down a few Kleenexes from the trunk, but it was pointless—Jennings was gushing. I reluctantly helped him into the car and winced at the blood pooling on the seat. Just like that, we went canoodling off to see Uncle Phil.

"You saw him pull the gun on me—why didn't you do something?!" Jennings roared.

"You think I'd risk a stray bullet ending my career?"

Within minutes of arriving, Jennings had been stowed in the maternity ward, where he remained hidden from the public eye. Phil personally stitched Jennings's scrotum together, and lo and behold, Jennings got his hose unkinked that night. Six years later, Jennings married Monica Lewis, the original Chiquita Banana, with whom he had two beautiful children. Apparently my lineage serves well for doctors as well as executives—Phil kept everything in working order.

Once Jennings got back in the saddle, he went on the hunt for Walter Wanger. Though Joan denied her affair with Jennings and asked that her husband be absolved of all charges, Jennings was thirsty for blood. Wanger hired Jerry Giesler, the world's highest-paid attorney, whose client list included Marilyn Monroe, Charlie Chaplin, Bugsy Siegel, and Alexander Pantages. Pleading a temporary insanity case, Giesler mounted the defense of a lifetime, getting Wanger's sentence reduced to four months in a soft jail. In a career that extended thirteen more years, Wanger went on to produce massive studio titles including Cleopatra.

When MCA's owner, Jules Stein, heard about the whole mess, he called business affairs to prepare Jennings's severance documents. But Lew Wasserman, the president of MCA, glided in to save his employee. After all, Jennings Lang was bright; he just couldn't keep his cock in his pants.

I was glad to see that everyone fared well after the debacle, but to my misfortune, I was the guy whose car interior had been ruined. I tried to blot out the stains of Jennings's scrotal blood, but I was unsuccessful. So, I tooled off to the old-fashioned car wash on Pico and Beverly Glen and asked the attendant for a full scrub of the upholstery. When the attendant saw the mess, he scurried off and grabbed the owner, who was equally shocked.

"There's a lot of blood on your seat, sir," he said slowly.

"I get terrible nose bleeds. Dry season," I replied.

"It's smeared into the leather. I'm going to have to report this to the authorities." The last thing my career needed was a scandal, so I slipped the owner a five-dollar bill.

"I was the good guy in this scenario," I said. The owner looked at the bill in his palm for a moment, then folded it in half and pocketed it.

"It'll be ready in a half hour."

And just like that, the Jennings Lang scandal was laid to rest.

Discretion is everything.

What would have happened if news broke about Jennings Lang's casual encounters? For one, MCA would have lost Joan Bennett as a client, but that'd be nothing against the PR tornado that would have swept across the agency. In a business founded on appearances, sometimes you need to hold some details back. That isn't to say that I endorse lying—in fact, I'm of the mind that futzing with the truth always comes back to bite you in the rear end. But my career has taught me to be judicious and strategic with the details. This idea translates to the creative sphere as well. How many terrible movies have fantastic trailers? Studios pour bags of money into marketing teams that cut dragging plotlines and tedious dialogue. The point is this: even if you have an Oscar-worthy film, an Emmy-worthy television show, or a sterling track record as an executive, be careful with the information that you release into the world.

When I was six years old, my mother's case of hay fever sent the Katleman family crawling from Nebraska to California. We landed in the city as a pack of strays with a little money and no meaningful relationships. Like college students flocking to California schools, we were here for the weather.

There were four men of the Katleman family: Michael, Maurice, Carl, and Jake. Michael, my father, worked as a manager for Uncle Maurice, who built a modest parking lot business. Carl was an attorney who helped the famous priest Father Flanagan establish Boys Town, one of the best orphanages in the country. Uncle Jake tapped the gambling business as a bookmaker and ultimately bought the El Rancho Casino in Las Vegas. With a less-than-loose affiliation with the Jewish Mafia, Jake was ambitious, well connected, and, above all else, tough. His naturally gentle demeanor was prone to shattering in the blink of an eye. I remember casting bets on the UCLA-USC football game outside the Los Angeles Coliseum when a sailor bumped into Jake and mumbled, "Get out of the way, you kike." Next thing I knew, he had cocked his .38 Smith and Wesson, and my father and Uncle Maurice were trying to hold him down. Jake was not someone you messed with if you wanted to collect Social Security.

At least once a month, Uncle Jake would invite the infamous mob boss Benjamin "Bugsy" Siegel to a helping of my mother's brisket and potato pancakes. Bugsy, of course, was the quintessential celebrity assassin who proved instrumental in the development of the Las Vegas Strip.

"Call him Benjamin if you value your future," Jake muttered to me after I shook Bugsy's hand for the first time.

Somehow, our dinner table became a resting spot for a whole slew of roughnecks, including Bugsy's crony Mickey Cohen. As I was just a teenager and averse to the business of killing men, I would sneak away to my bed as soon as I could. But not before Bugsy had the chance to hand me a twenty-dollar bill and administer a key piece of advice: "If she's cute, wear protection."

With the exception of Jake's nefarious business contacts, we were a speck among the city's countless Jewish families. The entertainment industry siphons itself off from the rest of the world, including the majority of Los Angeles. Growing up, my only window into show business was through my father's high-stakes poker game, which included Jack Warner, founder of Warner Bros.; Louis B. Mayer, founder of MGM; and Harry Cohn, founder of Columbia Pictures. By contrast, Michael Katleman was a parking lot manager with a salary of one hundred dollars per week. Luckily, Uncle Jake had the bank account to back him.

On Saturday afternoons, my father would drop me off at the movie theater to catch a matinee. Then he would head to the poker table in the office of Myron Selznick, the powerhouse agent and brother to famed producer David O. Selznick. Once my movie let out, I would walk over to Selznick's office and draw a chair behind my father as he took on the heavy hitters.

"Do not open your mouth," he muttered to me. "Observe."

My father lost twice in five years. His lacking of a silver spoon didn't matter; at the poker table, he made short work of the entertainment moguls. Watching him play taught me a lot more than poker; it taught me how to go up against bulldogs.

Despite my father's gambling prowess, we weren't a blip on Hollywood's radar. Although I was raised within a five-mile radius of the Hollywood sign, I wasn't close to the stars until I got my first break at MCA, the dominant talent agency of that era. But once I accessed the industry's underbelly, I learned the irony of it all.

Most moguls are immigrants to the business.

If you think that the entertainment business is comprised of entitled fat cats sitting in their ivory towers. . . well, you might be partially right. But even the most bourgeois of executives didn't start out that way. There's a film of nepotism in any high-profile industry, but most of the people who make it in show business weren't born with a pedigree card. Instead, they took great measures to forge cards for themselves. If you believe that someone was born into the lap of luxury, you've probably bought into their illusion. Let's not overlook the blatant lack of diversity in the business; no one can deny that white men have a major advantage over women and minority races. That's a problem that needs to be addressed at every level of the industry. But I think there's a fallacious mind-set that the people who make it in the entertainment business were born successful, and that's just simply not the case.

This is all to say: if you think you can't access the industry because you were born with a rusty spoon, you're wrong. Yes, it's an industry of relationships; yes, you need a connection to get in; and yes, it takes luck to rise to the top. But if you want it bad enough, it's possible. You just need to be resourceful.

The Music Corporation of America (MCA) trickled out of Chicago in the fervor of Prohibition. Its leader was Jules Stein, the prolific ophthalmologist who treated glaucoma by day and scouted for hot bands at night. Jules was a scientist at the surface but a jazzman at heart. He had managerial features—a wooden block of a chin, no lips, and thin, white hair pasted back about his crown. I never saw him wearing anything other than a double-breasted charcoal suit with a pocket square. He didn't look like other entertainment executives—Jules never had any grease to him. Even after his success in show business, he was always a doctor.

A fledgling saxophonist and violinist, Jules slogged through his college tuition bills by playing bar mitzvahs and small weddings. After realizing he couldn't blow, pluck, or fiddle, he turned his focus to ophthalmology. But that didn't stop Jules from immersing himself in the heart of Chicago's music scene, lending his ear to local jazz and ragtime talents. He started booking gigs for performers around the city as his relationships with artists and venues began to proliferate. When Prohibition jarred Chicago's music scene and lent for the rise of the speakeasy, Jules hit a gold mine. The countrywide ban on alcohol provided the key element for entertainment to thrive: exclusivity. Before Prohibition, Jules's performers were average joes singing into the wind—folks you could find on any given night. But now you had to sneak your way into seeing them. Watching a performance was legally forbidden yet culturally possible, and the mystique behind the music scene skyrocketed. Benefiting from it all was the wire-jawed Jules Stein, hiding under his lab coat at the local eye clinic.

Once Jules shook hands with a man called Alphonse Capone, his underground business grew into a small empire. Primed as the monarch of Chicago's music scene and the gatekeeper to the city's talent, Jules was invaluable to moonshining tycoons who needed live performers at their speakeasies. But Jules had aspirations beyond the haunts and clubs of Chicago. He cared about culture and spectacle, and that meant tapping the film business. Jules called his company MCA and packed his bags for Beverly Hills.

When he arrived in the desert, Jules built his headquarters at 360 Crescent Drive, one block south of Santa Monica Boulevard. And who better to design the complex than the legendary African American architect to the stars, Paul R. Williams. In addition to designing the iconic Beverly Hills Hotel and Al Jolson's triumphant tomb at Hillside Memorial Park, Williams designed homes for larger-than-life figures like Frank Sinatra and Lucille Ball.

Williams mapped the complex with a southern, colonial style that oozed of old money. Within months, he had erected the nerve center of MCA, equipped with iron gates, gardens, fountains, and spiral staircases. The interior housed over thirty offices, a projection room, and a secret bar. It ensured that Hollywood's brightest stars, along with the agents who wrangled their careers, felt comfortable and esteemed. Unlike the city in which it was built, the building wasn't a facade—it was furnished with antique desks and artifacts that Jules sold for millions when MCA moved to the Universal lot decades later. Everyone within the office was terrified of spilling ink or scuffing the priceless woodwork. And if an agent left any stray papers or personal belongings out, he'd be greeted the following morning with a strongly worded note from MCA's founder.

Amid a town of excess, I never observed a vice in Jules Stein. His wife, Doris, was piss-elegant, his pair of daughters and sons behaved like ushers, and his business acumen was tight and sensible. Jules was a sober man, capable of grounding a burgeoning company with reason and leadership.

Two decades later, his agency came to thwart other representative giants like William Morris and Famous Artists. In purchasing the rival agency Hayward Devrage, MCA expanded into television, theater, and motion pictures, representing the best performers, producers, writers, and filmmakers in the world. The agency had an all-star cast of agents who covered the town, led by the inscrutable super agent Lew Wasserman as president.

Meanwhile, yours truly had moved on from his job as an ice deliveryman in favor of taking classes at UCLA. After I wrapped my classwork in June, I found myself looking for jobs in the city. The most obvious man to approach was Uncle Jake. At first, he offered me a job at the El Rancho, but I had no desire to make a living out of Las Vegas's underworld. Nothing ventured, nothing gained—I told Jake that I wanted to stay in Los Angeles.

"Well," Jake said, "ever think about the agency business?"

It turns out that Nat Devrage, the co-founder of Hayward Devrage, was an action junkie who would bet on anything including two snails sliming up a window. Needless to say, he had a fast friendship with Jake, who got me an interview at MCA. At that point I hadn't seriously considered what I would do for a living. My father encouraged me to sell appliances at Sears on account of their employee pension program, but I wasn't precious on memorizing the specs of the latest and greatest washing machines. My sliver into MCA was my first glimpse at a life—not an education with a four-year expiration date, not a connection—but an industry that could allow me to exceed the expectations I had set for myself. With Jake's connection to Nat and my ability to flap my gums, I knew I was a shoo-in, barring the chance I get sick in the room. The only obstacle between me and MCA was a suit.

MCA mandated an antiseptic attire: white shirt, black suit, black knit tie, black socks, and black shoes. If your sideburns weren't clipped or you left a patch of scruff on your face, the office manager would send you straight to the barber. In fact, as an agent years later, I made the mistake of coming in on the weekend wearing a blue blazer, gray slacks, and a bow tie. When Lew Wasserman snagged a glance at me, he made it clear that the only man permitted to wear a bow tie at MCA was named Frank Sinatra. Then he directed me to the closest men's clothing store.

Find a way to look the part, even if you can't afford it.

As the halfback of my high school football team, I'd never had any reason to dress like a gentleman. I had walked through life wearing a letterman's jacket, corduroys, and sneakers. But Jake made it clear to me—I couldn't show up at MCA looking like a college jock. That lesson applies to every corner of Hollywood. When the cameras are always flashing, you better be ready to have your picture taken.

With no money to spare, my parents and I spent a Saturday morning at the Bank of America on Beverly and Wilshire, where I got a $200 loan to buy two suits. My bottom-of-the-barrel salary allowed me to pay it off at $10 a month. And just like that, with a little debt and a lot of luck, I was ready to make a name for myself in Hollywood.

I had never seen the sights of London, Rome, or Paris, but as I walked through the iron gates of MCA, I was convinced that this place dwarfed any European monument. Mind you, I was nineteen years old and wearing a suit made out of cardboard that still belonged to the bank. The main doors of MCA opened to a foyer floored with black and white chess tiles. The walls were wainscoted and covered in eggshell paint, and a crystal chandelier jingled in the center of the room. The centerpiece was an ornate staircase that curled to the right, with mint-green carpet unfurling down the center of the steps and a mahogany strip of wood curled down the banister. The second story had three wings designated for each leader of the agency. Jules Stein's office loomed straight ahead, Taft Schreiber's veered off to the right, and Lew Wasserman's crouched in the right corner. I was not bound for any of these wings; upon checking in, I was promptly taken to the basement, where I sat with Paul Ramar, the office manager.

Here stood a man who shepherded countless young men through the ranks of the company without leaving the windowless mailroom. Needless to say, he was pricklier than a cactus. I managed to mix the right cocktail of earnestness and sangfroid, and within minutes Ramar offered me a summer internship. He had just one condition. Ramar was low on members for his bowling team, so I had to commit to rolling pins on Wednesday nights. He made it evidently clear that blowing a league game would lead to the ax.

Climbing the ranks of an agency is one of the sacred traditions of the business. Though there have been slight variations over the years, the basic structure was the same back then as it is today. New hires were given the title of office boy and planted in the bowels of the mailroom, where they sorted mail and maneuvered the carts. In the tumult of the agency's hierarchy, office boys were expected to start at the bottom of the food chain and work their way up. Office boys made sure that everything—contracts, films, fan mail—reached its intended executive without fail. In between the sorting process, they were on call for any grunt work that an assistant might have. The wage was $50 a week, and the agency gave Sundays off.

As positions arose, an agent would reach into the pool of office boys and handpick someone as his assistant. Assistants were accountable for everything in an agent's life, professional and personal tasks included.

They took dictation, listened on each call, and scheduled every meeting. The agency promoted its strongest oxen to junior agents within a few years. These young executives weren't tasked to sign new clients right away; they predominately leveraged jobs for the agency's preexisting clients. They called this servicing business covering. With success, the best covering agents got bumped to partner. These lucky veterans spoke with offer-clad executives and handled the careers of major stars behind their ornate desks.

I started out in the mailroom with a crop of nervous kids who believed they could rise to the top of the business. These were my friends and competitors, and I would have to beat them out for jobs as they arose. There were twelve of us; about one-fifth would be fired within the coming months—not because they were dense or unqualified, but because they misheard an agent saying he wanted two instead of three shakes of vanilla powder in his latte. Among others, one of my comrades who survived the scythe was Jerry Perenchio, the billionaire and former CEO of Univision.

During my second week in the mailroom, the starlet Joan Crawford had a major scuffle with the founder of Warner Bros., Jack Warner. This was the 1950s, when studio executives were terrified of the increasingly popular television set. The motion picture business had reason to fret— television programming threatened box office profits in a major way. So when Joan, who had signed a three-picture deal at the studio, requested a state-of-the-art television set in her dressing room, Jack went nuclear. He warned Joan to never broach the subject again if she wanted any future in show business. As one might predict, Joan had a meltdown and walked off the lot. MCA had no choice but to defend its A-lister. Jules Stein and Lew Wasserman tried to salvage the relationship with Warner Bros., but Jack wasn't one to be swayed. He banned all MCA agents from entering the Warner Bros. lot until Joan caved. This move ruffled more feathers than the embargo on Cuba—it was utter war.

If you've ever wondered what kind of paperwork circulates when a studio bans an agency conglomerate, I can tell you. The business affairs department has to issue cease and desist letters to each of the agency's clients. How many clients did MCA represent, you might ask? Well, considering that notices needed to go to each band member that MCA represented, about ten thousand. And as the office boy, guess who had the pleasure of licking each stamp?

After eight hours of slobbering over stale adhesive, I decided that enough was enough. Coincidentally, I had a loose affiliation with the agency's treasurer, Karl Kramer, as I had dated his daughter Louise. So I sidled up to Kramer and asked him if the mailroom had a Pitney Bowes stamp machine. He looked at me as if I was speaking French.

"What's the matter—is your tongue worn out?"

I wet my mouth with a sip of water and got back to work.

About one month into the job, Lew Wasserman's secretary, Shirley Kahn, asked if I would stop by Nate 'N Al's each morning to pick up a bagel and cream cheese for her. Of course I obliged with a pumpkin grin. As a teenager absorbing the shuffle of the agency's hierarchy, I didn't know much; however, it was impossible to miss that Lew Wasserman was a larger-than-life figure. Though Jules Stein had founded the company, Lew wore the keys on his belt. As president of MCA, he ran the company on a day to day basis, inventing booking strategies, helming a colossal talent roster, and leading MCA's team of agents. He ran the business like Apple or Google, looking ten years into the future. I bought and delivered that bagel each morning with more pride than I ever had for my education. They say that none of us are distanced from one another by more than six degrees of separation—I had only one between me and Wasserman. Two weeks later, Shirley asked if I'd be interested in becoming his assistant.

"Who do I have to kill?" I asked.

"Just show up at his place tomorrow morning. Eight a.m. sharp."

"I drive a 1936 Ford. Is that okay?" I asked.

"You'll be using his car," Shirley chuckled.

Apparently Lew had received six speeding tickets driving to Palm Springs, which had led to a six-month driver's license suspension. I would soon realize that I wasn't his assistant; I was his chauffeur.

Don't scoff at a chance to hit a homer.

No one likes sitting at the bottom of the food chain. Personally, my short stint in the mailroom drove me nuts, and I was a college dropout. I can only imagine what it's like to pore through dirty fan mail and push a gimpy cart with a graduate degree like so many budding prospects in the business. When you're balancing a dozen macchiatos, picking up dry cleaning, or holding someone's cigarette while they're taking a leak, it's impossible to not feel like you're wasting your life.

But so many people on the bottom rung forget that they've made it onto the ladder. It doesn't matter if you're handing out Christmas bonuses or pushing a dolly; if you can wedge your way into the heart of a studio, production company, or agency, you have a chance to make an impact. Bitterness about one's standing in the business blinds a person to the value of connectivity to the highest echelons of the business. At MCA, the letters, papers, and magazines that I delivered weren't mail— they were opportunities to make an impression on someone who could change my life with the nod of a head.

Nowadays, as the business is becoming increasingly corporate and more people are flooding to Hollywood, it's harder than ever to climb the ranks of a reputable company. That means a greater number of assistants are doing coffee runs into their late twenties. . . and that's okay. If you fall into this category, try to avoid ruing the day you moved to Hollywood. Rather, take advantage of the platform you have in the company that employs you. A savvy, plugged-in assistant has the power to disrupt the whole business.

The following Monday, I pulled up to Lew Wasserman's house on Alta and Santa Monica Boulevard. I parked my Ford beyond eyeshot of the windows and walked toward the entry, trying to avoid sweating through my undershirt. With a deep breath, I cocked my wrist and gave the door three firm raps.

Though I had been at MCA for just over a month, I had never gotten a solid look at Wasserman. He was a trim man; his custom suits draped snugly over his body like clothes on a hanger. Though he had a tall stature, he was not an athlete. I imagine that without the bells and whistles of his attire, one might call him gangly. Whereas Jules Stein propagated a sense of class and tradition, Lew Wasserman was smooth and refined—the quintessential agent. He slicked his salt-and-pepper hair in a manicured wave and never let a thread fall out of place. Perhaps most striking were his glasses—thick, rounded frames with massive, shell-like lenses.

"What's your name?" Wasserman asked me.

"Harris Katleman," I responded.

"It's a pleasure, Harris. I'm Lew."

He tossed me the keys to his black Cadillac, and off we went. With that, my career-long mentorship with Hollywood's last mogul began. As someone who had grown up in the city, I considered myself knowledgeable of the streets of Los Angeles. That notion was quickly disproved when I started driving Lew. He had studied every side street and back alley in the city to avoid thoroughfares. So like an old-fashioned traffic app, Lew used his left finger to point either right or left at any given crossroad. I found myself having to focus more on his pointer finger than the cars in front of me as I meandered down streets I never knew existed. But we seemed to outflank traffic, and I refrained from crashing Lew's Cadillac into any signposts.

Though I would learn he had the ability to fly off the handle, Lew typically withheld a respectful, composed, and humble demeanor. People were nervous to call Jules Stein Jules, but you could most certainly call Lew Lew. Each morning I knocked on his door at 8:00 a.m. and chauffeured him to studios, production companies, and restaurants before dropping him off at his house once the sun had set. While he worked at his desk, I wrote up memos and booking slips for all of his deals. With zero legal experience, I didn't understand the terms that determined revenue, and screwing up meant clients not getting their money. More, I had a tough time making out Lew's chicken-scratch notes. After being tasked to invoice for a particularly large payment, I asked Lew to verify the deal memo I had written. I took a verbal beating for that one—Lew didn't want to do my job for me. I learned quickly that asking questions reflects weakness. Especially dealing with someone of Lew's level, I endeavored to keep my mouth shut.

As a fly on the wall, I observed the new ways in which Lew monetized the business. He knew that Hollywood doesn't exist to generate entertainment; it exists to generate money using entertainment as its medium. One afternoon, Lew received an unusual call from Bill Goetz, the president of Universal Studios. Bill had a lot of power and a composed disposition, but listening on the line, I could detect a shadow of desperation in his voice. He emphasized to Lew what we already knew: over the past few years, Universal had realized success with only two titles—*Ma and Pa Kettle* and *Francis the Talking Mule*—the latter of which had been kept on life support with tedious sequels and spinoffs. Bill was desperate for a hit, which meant he was desperate to cast stars. But with a string of failures at the box office, Universal was strapped for cash and unable to pay top dollar for prestige talent.

"You gotta help me, Lew," Bill kept repeating.

When Lew hung up, he turned to me and said softly, "I think I have an idea."

Lew and I riffled through Universal's projects in development, looking for a diamond in the rough. We stumbled upon *Winchester '73*, a Western with a strong leading role. With Lew's client James Stewart available, he deemed it the perfect fit. We sent the script to Jimmy, who fell in love with the project.

"How'd you like it if Jimmy Stewart played the lead in *Winchester '73*?" Lew asked Bill.

"That'd turn this whole boat around! How much does he cost?"

"He's free," Lew responded.

"What are you telling me?"

"I'm telling you that Jimmy Stewart will act in the movie for zero dollars. But he's going to need 50 percent of the film's profits."

"Half of the back end?"

"A movie starring Jimmy Stewart will make you millions," Lew said. "Let me know if we can close."

That afternoon, we got a revolutionary offer for Jimmy Stewart. For the first time in history, an actor would receive back-end royalties. The deal transformed the old-fashioned studio system by reallocating power from the studio to talent. As expected, the wrath of Hollywood rained down upon us. Lew got calls from every studio in town, but he didn't care. By not having to pay actor salaries, Universal rose to match MGM, and Lew had stolen the store for his clients.

That wouldn't be the only time that Lew leveraged his power to launch his clients' careers. An especially poignant example of his genius came years later, when Twentieth Century Fox decided to adapt the bestselling novel *The Young Lions* as a major motion picture. The legendary studio head Darryl Zanuck was hell-bent on securing Marlon Brando for the lead role—a proposition that Lew accepted on one condition.

"Marlon will do it, but he insists on having Dean Martin in the supporting role."

For context, Dean Martin had started out as a nightclub singer before becoming half of the Martin and Lewis comedy duo. He'd been haranguing Lew for an acting role for months, but casting departments wouldn't touch him with a ten-foot pole.

"This is a prestige picture," Zanuck responded. "I'm not hiring a nightclub singer."

"Okay. Marlon's out then."

"Come on, Lew. You can talk him into accepting someone else."

"Already tried. Why don't you try calling him? Here's his number. . . "

Well aware of Marlon's psychoses, Zanuck had no interest trying to reason with a loose cannon. Instead, he pounded sand and casted Dean Martin in the film. Of course Marlon couldn't have cared less if Dean Martin was in the film or not, but Zanuck would never find out. The real winner was Lew Wasserman, who quietly collected 10 percent of all client earnings. Not only that, *The Young Lions* launched an extremely lucrative acting career for Dean Martin.

Turn your opponents into marionettes.

Lew Wasserman had the uncanny ability of creating the illusion that the person across him held the power. In reality, he was always pulling the strings. Lew was able to make Bill Goetz feel *lucky* for inking the Jimmy Stewart deal. Not only did Lew get a boatload of money, he got an IOU from the president of Universal Studios.

If you're a bulldog in negotiations, you'll make a couple good deals and a ton of enemies. But if you can make the other side feel like they're winning, you'll open the door for future success.

When Lew asked me to accompany him on a business trip to New York, I figured I was being promoted from driver to travel associate. I didn't realize that I would be his acting anesthesiologist. Lew was terrified of flying, and if he wasn't knocked out when the plane left the tarmac, there would be hell to pay. Per his routine, Lew popped a sleeping pill the size of a small plum as we approached the gate, and he was out like a light within five minutes of boarding. The timing proved a bit too perfect as the plane was experiencing engine failure. After an hour, the pilot announced that the aircraft was unsafe for takeoff and passengers would have to make alternative travel plans. Anyone with eyes could tell that a sack of potatoes had a better chance of waking up than Lew did. We had no choice; the stewardess grabbed his wrists while I took hold of his ankles, and up the jet bridge we went. I managed to secure two tickets on the next flight that offered sleeping berths, and somehow we landed in time for Lew's dinner meeting. He was rather chipper after waking up with wheels on the ground.

"Not a bad flight, was it?" he remarked, unaware that he had come in on a separate plane.

When we returned to Los Angeles, Lew resumed his summer tradition of attending the Hollywood Park racetrack on Wednesdays. Top moguls like Jack Warner, Sam Goldwyn, Harry Cohn, and Bill Goetz had a crop of fine thoroughbreds that cost more than they ever won. Lew wasn't one to miss out on an event that attracted all the bigwigs of entertainment—he might have sealed more deals at the track than he did in boardrooms. Each week, he gave me $50 to throw at the nags that sparked my fancy. I pocketed every buck to pay off my suits. As I crowded around the turf club, paddock, and winner's circle, I felt the sizzle of privilege for the first time. No one knew I was a glorified summer intern when I was standing with the president of MCA.

My experiences with Lew and the ponies weren't always business related. In fact, we dipped into the Rolodex of my Uncle Jake when we encountered Sidney Korshak, the lawyer for the Chicago mob. Sidney had relationships with all the heavy hitters in town—Jules and Lew, Hugh Hefner, Frank Sinatra, Jerry Brown, Robert Evans—you name it. The FBI considered him "the most powerful lawyer in the world," and they were always trying to pin him. That precluded him from having an office—he returned incoming calls from phone booths around the city. One Wednesday, Korshak walked into the Turf Club with a group of unsavory characters. Deeming the racetrack a center of sophistication, the bourgeois owner Marje Everett tossed Korshak and his associates off the grounds.

"That's a mistake," Lew muttered as the crowd watched the spectacle.

Marje didn't take into account that Korshak represented the International Brotherhood of Teamsters, a major labor organization in the United States and Canada. The next day, the Teamsters incited a massive strike on Hollywood Park, and the gambling hub grinded to a screeching halt. It turns out that every track employee was a Teamster—the cashiers, the parking lot attendants, the horse handlers. Sidney had single-handedly shut the track down, which meant millions of Marje Everett's dollars swirling down the drain. When Sidney indicated no sign of mercy, Marje sought Lew's help. He had an affinity for Marje and promised to do what he could.

"What'll it take for you to lift the strike?" he asked Sidney, who listened from a pay phone.

"She's gonna have to come to my house and personally apologize."

That was Sidney's mandate—he had drawn his line in the sand. When we told Marje the terms, she promptly refused. But after a few more days of hemorrhaging money, Marje drove to Sidney Korshak's home in Bel Air and gave an Oscar-worthy "I'm sorry" speech. The track attendees were back at work the following day.

In addition to betting on ponies, Lew held a gin rummy game every weekend that included the likes of Sam Briskin, the president of Columbia Pictures; Louis Mayer, the founder of MGM; David May, the founder of May Department Stores; Cubby Broccoli, the producer of the Bond films; and Greg Bautzer, the industry's top entertainment attorney. Every Monday after the game, Lew would hand me massive checks from his winnings. He won so consistently that I asked him if he ever exercised his talents in Vegas.

"If Jules Stein found out that I pulled a Vegas slot," Lew said icily, "he'd have security escort me out of the building for good."

Before Lew had made his fortune, he lost a sum of $60,000 shooting dice in Vegas. Stuck in casino purgatory, he begged Jules for a bailout. Jules had commissioned a mole to hand deliver a check covering the debt on the sole condition that Lew never set foot in a Las Vegas casino. Lew kept that promise to his grave.

Everyone has a vice.

Even someone as smooth and powerful as Lew Wasserman has some dodgy tendencies to hide. Mine involved a string of marriages that all ended with divorce papers. At any rate, it's important to remember that your mentors aren't superhuman—they're human beings with flaws like everyone else.

⚙

I went into that summer allured by the idea of show business, and I came out addicted to the entertainment industry. The perks, the personalities, the glamour—I'd been bitten by the Hollywood bug. More, it occurred to me that entertainment was the only prestige industry that didn't require an investment to begin. Unlike fields like medicine or law that demand years of study, entertainment gave me a chance to play ball straightaway. I didn't have the appetite to return to a life of chasing girls at UCLA—I had seen too much of the good life.

A week before my summer term at MCA was due to expire, I gathered the nerve to stride past Shirley Kahn and into Lew's office. He took a quick glance at me and knew immediately what was on my mind.

"I like you, Harris. Once you have your degree from UCLA, come work for me."

"I don't want to go back."

"Don't be stupid—college is a luxury that I never had. After I got my high school diploma, I had to work as a theater usher in Cleveland. Still have the embroidered vest."

"I know exactly where I want to go and how I endeavor to get there. I don't want to drop out of college—I just want to transfer to the University of MCA."

Lew thought it over and chewed his pencil. "Let me speak with your parents," he mumbled.

And so just like four months earlier, my family had to scrounge up money for a cardboard suit. This time it was for my father. He was a Nebraskan labor man through and through—I don't think he had worn a suit on his wedding day. I'll never forget squinting into the crevice of Lew's office through the crack in the door. The image of my parents sitting on leather chairs that cost more than they made in a month seared into my mind. Ten minutes later, the door swung wide, and my parents emerged alongside my mentor. They clasped hands; then, Lew turned to me.

"Your education begins now, Katleman."

When my father got beyond eyeshot of the building, he ripped off his suit like a dirty bandage and curled into his Dodge, eager to get back to the parking lots. With my parents' blessing, I had planted both feet in entertainment. No longer was I Lew's driver—I was his protégé.

My apprenticeship under Lew gave me the mind-set that anything was possible. As a full-time employee of the agency, I proposed to my girlfriend, Carole, whom I married one month after her high school graduation. She had been dating Peter Stone, the future Tony, Oscar, and Emmy-winning writer. But Peter wore thick glasses, and I was Lew Wasserman's assistant. No longer did I wait in Lew's annex between meetings; I was stationed at a desk in his office with access to every call. I was shocked by the star power that glazed his phone sheet. His contacts extended far past Hollywood; it seemed that Lew had friends in every arena worth inhabiting.

If you're a Los Angeles local, you'll recognize Howard Hughes from the 405 freeway off-ramp named after him. Or if you're well versed on eccentric billionaires, you've probably seen pictures of Howard hunkered down at the Beverly Hills Hotel with eight-inch fingernails and Kleenex boxes on his feet. Howard Hughes goes down in history as one of the most colorful industry moguls, balancing a passion for aviation with his ownership of RKO Studios. Years prior, Howard had asked Lew to help him sabotage the actress Terry Moore. Her Heisman Trophy–winning husband out of West Point had found out about Terry and Howard's affair, and he had beaten the wiry aviator to a pulp. Howard wanted revenge. When Lew looked into it, he found that the angry husband was Glenn Davis, an army man with a porcelain face. Lew kept his hands clean, telling Howard that he deserved to get throttled for sleeping with the wife of a real-life GI Joe.

Since then, Howard had thought up a grand business idea for Lew's client Jane Russell. Jane had just broken barriers with Howard's latest film *The Outlaw*, one of the first feature films to show cleavage. As anticipated, the public responded to racy screen images, and Hughes wanted to capitalize on the new market demand. His plan: design a "super-brassiere" to be made available for wide consumption. He was hell-bent on securing Jane Russell as the face, or rather the bosom, of his new product. So I followed the flick of Lew's left pointer finger through the streets of Los Angeles, en route to the billionaire who commercialized the aircraft industry.

Hughes had built a secret office in the bowels of Hollywood. The complex was unmarked and vomit green in color. The whole transaction felt eerie, almost illegal as I brought the dapper Lew Wasserman into the tycoon's lair.

The meeting got off to a tense start as the two men discussed figures for Jane's endorsement deal. Every third line or so, Hughes would interrupt Lew and ask him to repeat his last sentence. Howard had allegedly lost 70 percent of his hearing in a succession of near-fatal plane crashes, and by the end of the meeting, Lew was yelling into Hughes's face. The aviator had no problem dishing it back.

"It'll double the size of her breasts!" cried an agitated Hughes when Lew asked why the world's biggest star should commit to a certain style of underwear.

Lew walked out of that room with a ten-year deal worth $100,000 for Jane. It was a colossal price to pay back then, especially in a time when most deals had terms of three years. As we left, Lew started chuckling from the passenger seat.

"Howard isn't that hard of hearing," he said. "He plays the whole thing up. . . makes you yell in his ear. You know why? Because he wants to make sure you aren't lying. No one lies when they're shouting.

No one lies when they're shouting.

Don't let his Kleenex boxes and long fingernails fool you—Howard Hughes was a wise man. I don't know if he learned this one from Sigmund Freud or Carl Jung, but it's as close to foolproof as anything I've ever picked up. I wouldn't classify myself as a hothead, but I used shouting as a lie detector countless times throughout my five decades in entertainment. If you ever suspect that someone's pulling the wool over your eyes, turn up the heat a little and see how the person reacts. If they crumble, they're lying.

Lew's Rolodex extended past moguls like Howard Hughes and into politics. When John F. Kennedy was running for president of the United States, we received an incoming call from Bobby Kennedy, who asked to meet with the powers of MCA. Lew obliged, and within a week I was in a room with Lew, Taft Schreiber, Jules Stein, and Bobby Kennedy. Bobby was looking for political endorsements that would carry weight to the rest of America.

"If you can get Hollywood to back Jack," Bobby said measuredly, "we'll owe you forever." Lew smiled and leaned forward in his chair.

"No problem, Bobby."

Jules had purposefully structured MCA to reflect clients' political beliefs. That way, the company could temper potentially isolating ideologies of die-hard clients. Taft Schreiber appealed to Republicans, while Lew was fiercely liberal. To that effect, Lew took charge of securing Kennedy endorsements. He threw an A-list gala, which raised massive amounts of money for Kennedy.

Over a decade later, when Bobby Kennedy held the post of attorney general, MCA became the subject of an antitrust investigation. Kennedy had grown concerned that the company had acquired too much power and monopolized the marketplace. Lew reminded Bobby of single-handedly delivering innumerable votes to his brother. Supposedly, Bobby feigned a foggy memory and told Lew that the Kennedys didn't owe anything to MCA. So much for promises.

Bobby's charge against MCA ended the agency's representation business overnight. Lew requested time for the company to transition into other avenues, but that wasn't in the cards. In the blink of an eye, the executives of Hollywood's top agency found themselves scrambling for employment. George Chasin, Herman Citron, and Arthur Park, the co-heads of the motion picture department, managed to scrounge up the space and capital to form a splinter agency called Chasin-Park-Citron. They took a large portion of MCA's star clientele. The rest of MCA's talent were subject to the snapping jaws of the agency's competitors looking to bolster client lists.

Amid the uproar of signing campaigns, Lew used the attorney general's mandate to his advantage. In tandem with MCA's thriving Revue Studios, which produced a number of genre thrillers, comedies, and specials, MCA bought Universal Pictures and Decca Records with the aim of transitioning into production. Lew transformed Universal Studios into the largest and busiest lot in town, making the company more profitable than ever before. Regardless of the favorable outcome, Lew never forgot Bobby's treachery.

Working for Hollywood's most powerful salesman offered a priceless view into the clockwork of the business. I spent a year watching a master at work, whether he was entrenched in a high-stakes negotiation, making managerial decisions for the future of MCA, or boosting a needy client's ego. But sooner or later, all apprenticeships come to an end. It was time to contribute to the company not as Lew Wasserman's assistant, but as Harris Katleman. Though I suppose it was a promotion, becoming a junior agent felt like tumbling down several rungs. I was used to interfacing with top-level studio heads, network executives, and stars calling for Lew. Now, I had to generate business without a name or a reputation.

An Agent Is Born
1951–1962

As a newly minted agent, I found that there were two departments with openings: the band and act division and the literary division. My distaste for drugs and alcohol all but soiled my chances of success in the music business. That left the department responsible for adapting books to film. When my parents heard that their son who'd foregone a UCLA education for show business had become an agent in MCA's literary group, they practically spit out their coffee.

At the end of most days, my boss from hell, Ned Brown, would toss a set of galleys into my cubicle and demand a report by the following morning. The galleys were full-length manuscripts—most of which had yet to attract a publisher. In other words, they were stinkers. The mailroom printed the galleys and bound them with three golden brads. To this day, those golden pegs of metal give me the willies—they remind me of sleepless nights, trying to muster through tedious language and muddled storylines.

I didn't have the name to attract new signs, but I could add value by finding material to package with MCA's stout client roster. Our primary competitors—the William Morris Agency and Famous Artists—were putting a ton of energy into the literary business. That allowed them to generate material for filmmakers and talent, which they used to poach MCA clients. It was my job to counteract these rogue signing efforts by providing literary value internally. I consumed nothing but pure garbage for the first few months. As I lamented my difficulty finding worthwhile material, Lew gave me the best advice I could have asked for.

Don't judge it; sell it.

Whichever portion of the industry you're occupying, it's essential to know your role. Writers conjure stories, directors bring them into the world, executives distribute content—and agents, as Lew made expressly clear, *sell*. While they might have the loudest voice throughout a negotiation, agents are all but mute when it comes to the creative elements of a project. This realization ultimately drove my decision to leave the representation business. I had a hankering to shepherd the creative process, and that sure as hell wasn't going to happen at MCA.

Ultimately, the agency is a volume business where quantity supersedes quality. The best agents don't necessarily have the best taste; rather, they have a relentless nature that drives them to keep tapping at the door of studios and networks. In the world of sales, your batting average means nothing while your number of hits means everything. In any case, I learned my lesson: agents are pinch hitters. Swing enough times and you're bound to hit a home run.

I hit the jackpot with a novel called *From Here to Eternity*. Told from the perspective of an unknown World War II veteran, the story was absorbing and wrought for cinema. More, the book posed a real hero as its protagonist, and I knew that the role would attract top-grade MCA talent. With some hard-hitting artillery in my back pocket, I walked into Ned Brown's office the following morning with a comprehensive coverage report and a glowing review. After an uninspired glance at my recommendation, he uttered with molasses in his voice, "Who wants to see another war story? Dump it."

What was the point of slaving over dense texts if I didn't have the power to do anything with them? I left Ned's office fuming and determined that I would have to slip through his grip. At that juncture, I had been assigned to cover Columbia Pictures, and I pinpointed the young producer Buddy Adler as a key studio contact who might spark to the book. One evening as I left the lot, I noticed he had a flat tire. This was my chance—I summoned the nerve to ask if he wanted a ride. On our way to Beverly Hills, I broached that I had found a dynamite book.

"I owe you for the ride—why don't you messenger me the galleys?" he said.

A year and a half later, *From Here to Eternity* won eight Academy Awards, including Best Picture, Best Writing, and Best Directing. Adler, whose flat tire ultimately led to a solid-gold statue in his office, sang my praises to Lew Wasserman, and my star went off the charts. Ned Brown tried to snag credit for packaging the title, but, I had proof of my involvement. *From Here to Eternity*'s author, James Jones, gifted me a first edition of the novel with the inscription: "For Harris, who's had more trouble with me than I'm worth." That package provided enough cause for the gods of MCA to bail me out of Ned Brown jail. I bade a happy farewell to overnight novel reads and rolled up my sleeves to work with actors, writers, and directors in the motion picture department. And more, the town was touting me as one of the young Turks at the agency.

The closer you get to the flame, the hotter you get.

An agent's value is determined by the quality of his or her clients—nothing more, and nothing less. This fact lends the industry its cutthroat nature—everyone is always scrambling to sign the brightest stars. When it's all going well and the industry is nibbling scraps from your palm, there isn't a better life out there. The reverse is just as true; a roster of burned-out clients is about as useful as a Ferrari with a broken axel.

Every Tuesday morning at seven o'clock, the motion picture department would meet in the MCA theater. One by one, we reviewed the studios as a group, milling through production slates and available jobs. These department meetings separated MCA from the white noise of other agencies. Any whack job can rent a building, get a business license, and sign naive clients. But MCA's relationships and connectivity attracted a wellspring of exclusive information to share on Tuesday mornings. Each meeting presented the opportunity to shine, as well as the possibility to get pinned. Though the company committed itself to a collaborative culture, I never let my shoulders down in that room. Sharks still bite, even if you're one of them.

The meetings were two-thirds business and one-third pep rally, which meant they cultivated friendships among the company's agents. Just a few years prior, I had viewed MCA agents as superstars while delivering their mail. Now, they were my colleagues. Jerry Gershman was a wry, smart executive who would lie out in traffic if it meant attracting business. In fact, he legally changed his surname from Gershman to Gershwin to trick people into thinking he was related to the composer George Gershwin. Other agents of note included the powerhouse duo Kay Brown and Phyllis Jackson, the first female agents in history. Representing literary giants like Dr. Seuss, Ian Fleming, and Arthur Miller, they curbed the misogynistic culture of Hollywood in a major way. Their counterpoint was the debonair cocksman Doug Whitney, who embodied the boys' club of 1950s Hollywood. I could see straightaway that Doug was a top-notch agent when dialed in, but his philandering pulled him away from the office. One Tuesday when Lew asked for an update on Columbia Pictures, Doug lied that he had met with the studio president Harry Cohn the week prior. The whole room shook when Lew erupted.

"No, you didn't—I spoke with Harry this morning, and he hasn't seen you in a month!"

Sharks bite other sharks.

When I was Lew Wasserman's office boy, I figured that being accepted into an elite circle of agents meant that I'd be able to tiptoe on water. That wasn't the case at MCA, and it isn't the case at today's powerful companies, either. As an assistant or a low-level associate, you might get crushed for benign errors like botching a coffee order or screwing up an email. But once you get some power in the business, you can do some real damage. And that results in being pulverized by the leaders of the business. Regardless of status, I suppose that getting bitten is part of any legitimate industry.

✳

That isn't to say that some of the verbal beatings from MCA royalty weren't warranted. I remember Ray Sackheim, a colleague who covered a struggling production outfit called Republic Pictures, faced serious trouble when the studio head Herbert Yates submitted an offer to Joan Crawford to star in one of his C-level films. The first rule of representation involves understanding client egos. Telling a star—especially a star like Joan Crawford—to engage with a project "beneath" her is the perfect ticket to getting fired. But Ray was afraid of passing without Joan's consent, so he sent her the script and offer.

Lo and behold, Joan went off like a bomb, imploring Lew why her agency wanted to ruin her image and career path. Lew managed to talk Joan off the cliff, but he gave me strict orders to fire Ray. Now it was Lew who needed calming down—I defended my friend and prevented security from escorting him out of the building. But when Ray made the same mistake with Randolph Scott within the year, I couldn't protect him from the jaws of human resources. As Albert Einstein claimed, the definition of insanity is repeating the same action and expecting different results. It just goes to show—in Hollywood, image and reputation are your only currency. The money comes secondary.

I suppose the irony of Hollywood feeds upon the fact that sometimes there is no right answer. A few months after Ray left MCA, the television producer Don Fedderson submitted an offer for Fred MacMurray to star in a comedy about a single father's struggle to raise his children. Certainly not a project fit for a major film star. Respecting the producer's need to cast the pilot, I told Fedderson not to waste his time on Fred. He must have been well versed in black magic or hypnosis, because he convinced Fred to play the leading role. Brewing over my lack of support, Fedderson made sure to emphasize MCA's supposed incompetence to Fred. I knew I was cooked when the series ballooned into the award-winning hit *My Three Sons*, which went on for twelve seasons. Fred fired the agency, and I stood in the crosshairs. I expected Lew to splash acid on my face, but instead he offered me grounded feedback.

"Don't hold an actor's meeting for him," Lew said. "Let him say no."

In hindsight, Lew's advice was obvious. You never know what's going to hit when you're faced with a mediocre script and a meager budget. But how was the MacMurray episode different from Ray's screwup with Joan Crawford? It all boils down to making every client feel like they're positioned at the center of the universe.

Despite my occasional rookie mistake, my growing presence at the agency earned me access to the parties that Jules Stein threw at his beautiful home in Beverly Hills. They were some of the city's most exclusive events; you couldn't grab a glass of wine without running into a major celebrity, politician, or company titan. Jules's residence, which was bought by Rupert and Anna Murdoch after Stein's death, epitomized tasteful extravagance. Jules had filled his home with an impressive collection of antique ladders—what better symbolism for a man who climbed to the highest rung of entertainment. There must have been fourteen pieces of silver surrounding each plate in the sprawling dining room.

"Which fork do I use?" my wife, Carole, whispered in my ear once dinner was served.

"Watch the person across from you," I muttered back, trying to act normal.

But the pinnacle of MCA excess occurred during the holiday season, when the company indulged an orgy of client egos. I hadn't known it as an assistant, but a committee comprised of Stein, Wasserman, and the heads of the motion picture, television, and band and act departments split clients into A, B, and C lists for the purposes of designating gifts. What did

Santa have in the bag for the A-listers? Black Cadillacs with leather interior. Needless to say, these lists were locked up tighter than Fort Knox. B- or C-level clients could never find out that they hadn't made it onto the A-list. The gift-giving process didn't derive from anything related to generosity. Lew and Jules knew their clients were targeted by competing agencies, and they needed to make physical expressions of goodwill. It was a client-retention strategy—a defensive maneuver to lock down Hollywood's talents.

"Actors aren't picked for their brains," Lew told me. "And the word *loyalty* isn't in their vocabulary."

Treat every creative like they're Bill Shakespeare.

In a business that's completely reliant on the genius of others, I can't stress the importance of tending to client relationships. Even the most powerful agents are nothing without their clients' loyalty. In other words, there's always the chance that your star might get spun by the charms of another agent. Remember that Hollywood doesn't offer any insurance. If you don't spoil your clients rotten, the whole charade can come crashing down.

In addition to distributing gifts, Jules made his presence known at the many high-profile parties across Los Angeles. His transportation option was an off-duty ambulance that swapped out gurneys for red booths with bottles of champagne and caviar. After the Steins piled through the double doors, their driver would flip on his sirens and take them blaring off toward their next party. Anything to beat holiday traffic.

The holiday festivities were a vital perk, but to my dismay I'd be exiled from Los Angeles at the urging of Lew Wasserman. In the new year, Lew called me into his office wearing a particularly grim shape on his mouth.

"How would you like to live in New York?" he asked.

I hadn't climbed the ranks of the agency to be punted out of Hollywood and into the cold of the eastern seaboard, but I could tell that

Lew was administering more of a mandate than a request. As it turned out, the agents working out of the New York hub were running their own boutique agencies within MCA. Let's just say that they were feathering their own nests. Lew had gotten word, and he needed a bulldog to sniff out the clean agents from the crooked ones.

"I'm honored, Lew, but I have to be candid—I just got married, and I'm not sure my wife will support a move across the country."

"Then get a wife who will. MCA is your mistress."

"What will my title be?" I asked.

"Head of the television literary packaging department. Sound okay to you?"

That did it for me. I knew I had to abandon a work-life balance and the comfort of my home to excel in the business. So with twenty-three years under my belt, I flew my eighteen-year-old wife to the Big Apple, where we were greeted with a full-time car and driver.

Now, on my salary that paid $500 per week, Carole and I were living the lives of millionaires in an apartment that cost $3,000 per month—all expenses paid by MCA. Our neighbors included famed Broadway producer Leland Hayward and the president of Chase Bank, along with a smattering of other CEOs. It would suffice to say that our social circles didn't overlap. One weekend as I returned to the apartment after a run, one of our neighbors asked me if I was visiting my parents.

A similar welcome awaited me at the office. Entering a rogue fiefdom, I was resented for being Lew Wasserman's muscle. Even Sonny Werblin, the head of the East Coast office, who later owned the New York Jets, soured toward me as I first settled in. But as John Paul Jones said, "Damn the torpedoes, full steam ahead."

Though the prospect of firing agents twice my age daunted me, I knew that seasoned executives have a knack for smelling fear on weak men. Over the course of several months, I dismissed several agents, including David Susskind, who went on to host a self-titled talk show, and David Begelman, the future CEO of Columbia Pictures. When I entered Susskind's office to tell him that the company would not tolerate his unethical business practices, he looked deep into the grooves of my face.

"You can't fire me—you're just a punk kid." He promptly dialed Lew, who told him that the punk kid in his office was the ax and that he better pack his things before security throw his ass on the curb.

Never answer the birthday question.

I mean, there's just no good that can come from it. That goes for both business and romantic relationships—you never know what the magic age might be for an employer or a partner, so you might as well zip it. Plus, age doesn't really matter. I've dealt with executives in their twenties who think like seasoned moguls as well as blue hairs who never grasped how the business operates.

Sure, the fraudulent partners at MCA were pissed by my lack of crow's-feet when I fired them, but could you imagine if they knew that I was younger than most of their children? Having ripened over the years, I can speak from experience when I say that the old bull hates to be confronted by the young calf. The same principle applies on the other side of your early forties. At a certain point, CEOs are looking to hire the young guns who might flip the industry on its head, and that means trouble for the veterans with high cholesterol and varicose veins.

This notion is even more applicable in today's climate, as the profile of the executive is changing. Rather than the wide-lapeled mogul with cigar smoke on his breath, the business is starting to favor a new crop of people—Wall Street executives wearing rimless glasses, Silicon Valley types in turtlenecks, you name it. Ultimately, you want to be judged by your ability, not by an arbitrary number.

I wasn't winning any popularity contests, but the division showed a profit, and my bonus reflected it. Now it was time for me to start generating dollars for the company. There are several competing philosophies in the signing business, but any agent worth a damn would agree that defining a client roster is tantamount to success. Cultivating a client base involves building a brand. Many agents are looking for the big kahuna—a movie star with international value. These clients are lucrative, sexy, and utterly bonkers most of the time. Other representatives believe in the director business, as filmmakers have more longevity and creative control than actors. I operated under the philosophy that representing writers is the path to the promised land. Writers have the only Hollywood minds that can create something out of nothing. They're self-generating beasts; while actors and directors are perpetually pining for work, writers can scrawl their way out of unemployment. There's the added plus that they tend to be a bit more manageable than actors.

The only way to find writers whom I wanted to sign was to watch television shows until my eyes were ready to fall out. Bear in mind, all television was live—no tape, no VCRs, no internet. One night on an anthology series called the *Philco Television Playhouse*, I was taken by the writing of an episode titled "Marty." The writer, Paddy Chayefsky, agreed to meet with me on the sole condition that I buy him lunch. After a month-long full-court press, I secured my first sign by convincing Paddy that his episode carried feature film resonance. Now I had to deliver on that claim. My first step was to gain the support of Lew.

And so I recorded "Marty" using a kinescope—an old-fashioned television picture tube—and sent it to Lew via MCA's messenger service. Lew flipped for the show and encouraged me to shop the title around town. We attached Ernest Borgnine to star and Burt Lancaster's company to produce—the latter of which was an MCA client and generated a lucrative commission for the company. Paddy scribed a first-rate feature adaptation, and we were off to the races. The film version of *Marty* swept the twenty-eighth Academy Awards in 1955, picking up wins for

Best Picture, Best Director, Best Actor, and most importantly for me and Paddy, Best Writing. Paddy would grow into one of the most celebrated writers of our time, becoming the only writer to win three solo Academy Awards for Best Screenplay until Woody Allen.

Despite my wins for the company, my colleagues still viewed me as a smug prick. Come Labor Day, they neglected to invite Carole and me to their homes in the Hamptons. That was fine by me; I welcomed the idea of reclining in my fancy apartment without the pressure of being called into the office. The weekend would prove far from relaxing.

During that period, *The Jackie Gleason Show* was the number-one live event on the air. The president of CBS, Jack Van Volkenberg, had a closed-circuit feed to his apartment so he could watch every rehearsal. That Saturday, his wife decided to turn on the feed while entertaining her bridge group. Now, Jackie was known for his colorful language, which would put a longshoreman to shame, and Mrs. Van Volkenberg nearly fainted when she and her high-society friends heard the junk flowing from Jackie's lips. She dialed the control room and ordered Jackie to clean up his mouth. Krakatoa was second to Jackie's explosion. Unaware of being surveilled by the powers of CBS, he walked up to the camera and looked it square in the eye.

"Mrs. whoever you are—go fuck yourself and the horse you rode in on. You tape the show tonight—I'm out."

Remember, it was Labor Day weekend and no executive was anywhere close to the city. Even if they were, they sure weren't coming back to face Gleason. The only executive in town was yours truly, and I was dispatched to convince Jackie to return. Did I know Gleason? No, and he sure didn't know me. So off I went to the CBS soundstage, where I knocked on the door of Jackie's dressing room.

"Get the fuck out of here," Jackie barked. "I'll only talk to Wasserman."

"He's in LA and can't be reached," I responded.

"Then you'll have to get the bitch to tape the show."

"She wouldn't generate an eighth of the ratings you pull in," I said. "I'm

Harris Katleman, the head of the TV literary department." There was a sustained silence.

"Are you Jake Katleman's son?"

"He's my uncle," I said.

Jackie cracked the door and gestured toward a cushioned chair in his dressing room. Apparently my uncle had forgiven a gambling debt that Jackie had incurred at the El Rancho before becoming a star. Jackie said he'd return to the stage if I disconnected all cameras and had Mrs. Van Volkenberg personally apologize. When she refused, I had no choice but to tell Jack Van Volkenberg, one of the most powerful men in show business, that Jackie was hell-bent on suing his wife. I was flying by the seat of my pants, as I had no authority to make this threat. But Theodore Roosevelt's philosophy to walk softly and carry a big stick worked; Mrs. Van Volkenberg apologized, and Jackie graced the camera with his presence.

A "No" becomes a "Yes" when the right person asks.

I can only guess what would have happened to me if Uncle Jake hadn't forgiven Jackie Gleason's gambling debt. I probably would have failed to get him on the air, which would have been enough to have me promptly removed from my tentative seat of power. But as events transpired, Jackie requested that I be added to his agent team. Though I was still ensconced in New York and still not the flavor of the month, the Gleason episode won me the begrudging respect of my colleagues.

As I think on it, there was only a handful of people whose influence could have pulled Jackie Gleason out of his dressing room. That list didn't include Jack Van Volkenberg or yours truly, but it sure as hell included Jake Katleman. When you're trying to convince someone to do something, it's not just about how you present. . . it's about *who* presents.

In that era, the leading game-show producer was Goodson Todman Productions, the juggernaut that created *What's My Line?*, *Password*, *The Price Is Right*, and *Family Feud*. I received a call from Lew asking if I knew the owners, Mark Goodson and Bill Todman. Though Mark was coincidentally a cousin by marriage, I wasn't overly friendly with him. Lew told me to start forging a relationship with both men, as he wanted me to run point on a campaign to buy their company. This meant weekends at Westport, Connecticut, with Mark and Scarsdale, New York, with Bill. By the end of the summer, I broached that MCA was interested in buying Goodson Todman for $20 million. With inflation, that figure is equivalent to roughly $200 million in today's dollars. After weeks of negotiating, we arrived at an agreement of $25 million. I was over the moon, as were my superiors.

Lew and Jules boarded a flight bound for New York to ink the contract. But while they were in the air, Mark informed me that he and Bill had changed their minds. The deal was dead, and there was nothing I could do to resurrect it. I saw my career going up in smoke, and I had to leave for the airport to pick up Lew and Jules. At twenty-three years old, I had no idea how to break the news to my bosses. As I waited on the tarmac for their plane to touch down, I thought about feigning ignorance of Mark's call. In the limo ride to the doomed meeting, we could pop champagne and discuss my future at the company. Once Mark and Bill broke the news to Lew and Jules, I could flip the table in a frenzy, pretending they had pulled the wool over my eyes. It was an alluring idea, neglecting to face one's failure. But if I had learned anything during my tenure at MCA, it was that no one could bullshit Lew Wasserman.

When Lew and Jules exited the plane, I blurted that the deal was off. Jules seemed relieved, as it was all his money on the line, but Lew exploded. He insisted on meeting with Mark and Bill immediately. He was on the warpath from the instant the meeting started, throwing every argument into the wind. Mark and Bill wouldn't budge. The money was tempting, but they refused to answer to a parent company. After an hour of fruitless agenting, Lew made a final threat.

"If you don't sell, you'll be out of business in five years."

"We'll see about that." Mark smiled.

Sometimes, one boat simply isn't big enough for two parties.

I foresaw being transferred to the band and act department, which wasn't much better than being shipped to Siberia. Lew was frosty, but he kept me in charge of New York television. Still, I knew that I would have to pull off something glamorous to keep my star from flaming out.

As luck would have it, Harry Friedman, the MCA agent who covered MGM, suffered a nervous breakdown in Los Angeles. With the New York office's television department back on track, Lew summoned me to Beverly Hills to tag in for Harry. I was still the vice president of television, but at the age of twenty-six, my client list was about as short as my bank statement.

"I'm putting you on the team of my most temperamental clients," Lew told me. "That'll give you incentive to start signing."

That included a number of A-listers, including Grace Kelly, Fred MacMurray, Howard Keel, and future president of the United States Ronald Reagan. But the most notorious was none other than Marlon Brando, Hollywood's favorite mumbler. This wasn't the Marlon who waddled into the jungles of the Philippines one hundred pounds overweight to shoot *Apocalypse Now*, but he was certainly on his way. All the rumors about Marlon Brando's craziness are understated. He had a heart of gold and warm intentions, but the man couldn't sit alone in a room for five minutes without posing potential harm to his career. Marlon had recently come off the universal acclaim of *A Streetcar Named Desire* and was preparing to shoot a film called *The Wild One*. Along with my colleague Jay Kanter, I had to keep him out of trouble until principal photography commenced. Then it would be up to the director to wrangle him. Every evening after work, Jay and I babysat Marlon Brando at his house in the Hollywood Hills. Carole wasn't thrilled about me staying out past my bedtime, but I didn't have much of a choice.

Marlon, Jay, and I spent one evening—like most of the others—drinking mineral water and watching football. Around nine o'clock, he decided to turn in.

"I'm beat—gonna practice my lines in the mirror."

I figured that I'd wait a half hour before hitting the road, just to be safe. Within fifteen minutes, Marlon's house line rang. Lew Wasserman was at the other end of the line.

"Do you know where Marlon is?"

"Sleeping like a baby," I replied.

"Unless he's got a long-lost twin, I think you're mistaken. He just stumbled into Chasen's piss-drunk, with three women on his arm."

Jay and I bounded up the stairs and found a warm breeze pulsing through Marlon's bedroom. It was a scene out of a prison break movie. Marlon's bedsheets had been woven into a rope, secured to a radiator, and dropped out the window into the hedges below. I poked my head outside to find Marlon's vacant parking spot. When I thought about the wrath I could expect from Lew, I contemplated jumping from the window. But it was only the second story—I figured the fall would break my legs without killing me.

"Thanks a lot." Jay told Marlon the next day. "You're gonna get me and Harris fired."

"If those squares fire you, I'll leave MCA. Then you two can start your own agency with me as your first client."

"No, thanks," I said. "Then I'd have to watch after you for the rest of my life."

"That's the business you signed up for," Marlon said, shrugging.

Needless to say, I was eager to relieve myself of babysitting duties. That meant signing clients: big ones. How might a young agent steal A-level talent from other agencies, you might ask? The answer was covering studios. It was easy to make internal relationships within MCA. But building alliances across town—that was a far more difficult task, and perhaps the most important part of agenting. My covering assignments gave me an excuse to buddy up to meaningful executives and stars beyond the halls of MCA.

Harry Friedman's meltdown meant that I got to cover MGM: the holy grail of studios. Funding and releasing upper-crust titles like *The Wizard of Oz* and *Gone with the Wind*, their money flowed endlessly and they knew how to make smash hits.

"The sun never sets on the stars at MGM," people used to say, and they were right. MGM cast up their productions to the nines. Ensuring a strong presence on the lot would give me the best chance of poaching talent and building my name.

One afternoon at the MGM commissary, I managed to strike up a conversation with Clark Gable, the William Morris Agency's most important movie star. It was a bold move to sidle up to the King of Hollywood, but I figured that shame is for cowards. Clark mentioned that the Cove, Uncle Jake's club, was his favorite gambling den in Palm Springs. When I told Lew after a Monday staff meeting, he sicced me on Clark like a hound. Within a few weeks, I was sipping a glass of wine at Chasen's restaurant opposite Lew Wasserman and Clark Gable.

"You know, a guy like you," Lew drawled, "it's outrageous that you're making just $10,000 a week at MGM."

"I'm only making $7,500," Clark responded with a knife glint in his eye. Lew was astounded.

"What are they doing over there? If you sign with us, we'll double your salary. That's a promise." Clark got rather quiet after that. He was a brooding actor with an ego and a competitive streak. I could see the wheels turning in Clark's head.

After dinner, I was tasked to drive Lew home. I suppose an assistant's always an assistant.

"Who told you that Clark's getting ten grand a week?" I asked.

"The little bird inside my head. The key to building discontent is inflating expectation."

"If he comes over, how are we going to get him $15,000?"

"We'll cross that bridge when we get there."

Plan for the future and speak for the moment.

Clark Gable signed with us three months later. He was one of the first actors to get 50 percent of back-end profits on his movies, as derived by the deal structure that Lew had invented for Jimmy Stewart.

When you're dealing with fickle creative types, you have to ooze a sense of self-assuredness. While he was far from dense, Clark Gable was known for his mustache more than his business acumen. In order to motivate Clark to hitch his wagon to the MCA brand, Lew knew that he'd have to make some lofty claims. Some might call it flirting with deceit, but as an agent, you need to have the confidence to overpromise first and make things work later. Otherwise, you'll have a hard time assembling a meaningful client list.

⚙

Aside from using the studio lot as a melting pot, I found fresh talent by tracing leads from my clients. Creative people generally detect talent better than businesspeople can. Shortly after the Clark Gable sign, my writer Oliver Crawford introduced me to a guy he raved about. I was peeved to find that this supposed prodigy was a bartender at the Normandy named Nedrick Young. However, I valued Oliver's taste and read one of Ned's scripts that night. The story, titled *The Defiant Ones*, told the tale of two escaped prison convicts—one white and one black—chained to each other and forced on the run from the authorities. I sent the script to the famed producer Stanley Kramer, who expressed interest in directing. He offered to buy the script for $65,000. Mind you, that was quite a sum for a closet writer tending bar, but I figured I could get six figures for Ned's screenplay. I consulted Lew for advice, asking if I should settle for Stanley's offer or hold out for more money.

"Do you have sixty-five grand in the bank?" he asked. My answer was a resounding no. "Neither does Nedrick Young. Sell the damn script."

Stanley Kramer produced and directed *The Defiant Ones*, which starred Tony Curtis and Sidney Poitier. Ned won an Oscar for Best Original Screenplay and never had to dash bitters into cocktails at the Normandy again.

My next target was the legendary comic duo Dean Martin and Jerry Lewis, whom I had loved since watching *My Friend Irma*. After months of schmoozing, I proudly told Lew that Martin and Lewis were ready to sign.

"Do you know who represents those guys?" Lew asked.

"Abby Greshler," I replied.

"They're his only clients, Harris."

Lew had his assistant lob a call in to Greshler. I sat in awe as Abby took the call.

"Abby, we're in discussions with Martin and Lewis, and they want to leave your agency. How much commission do they generate for you over a five-year period?" Abby wasn't angry—he was crushed. We were taking his meal ticket. "We'll make sure you're taken care of," Lew said gently, before dropping the receiver.

That afternoon, Lew had a check for $1,000,000 messengered to Abby. People often deem Hollywood a bloody den void of ethics, but in my era there was honor among thieves.

Months later in one of our staff meetings, a colleague mentioned that Alfred Hitchcock's new project was in shambles. Hitchcock had hired and fired three different writers to crack the story. He didn't know what he wanted until someone brought it to him in silver wrapping paper, and the producers were beginning to think he was inconsolable. I pitched a young writer called John Michael Hayes, who was penning a radio show called *Johnny Dollar*. The senior agents laughed me out of the room for suggesting I set a meeting with Hitch, but I didn't care.

"It seems like you've all failed to date. I'll take the shot," I said. After the staff meeting, Lew grabbed my ear.

"You're on your own with this one. Hitch can go off like a loaded gun."

But I believed that John Michael Hayes could be the little writer that could, so I set the meeting with Hitchcock. To everyone's surprise, Hitch gave John the assignment to write a film called *Rear Window* at $1,000 per week. As John was used to writing one-hour radio shows in seven days, he finished the script in six weeks. Hitch refused to read it, insisting that John spend more time on it.

"Why don't you go to Palm Springs for three weeks and lie by the pool?" I suggested. "Submit the same draft once you get back."

John deemed the whole production silly, but he understood that Hitch had a challenging personality and willingly obliged. Hitch fell in love with John's draft and pushed it into production. After wasting a quarter-million dollars on three established writers who demanded competitive fees, Alfred Hitchcock got his script for $10,000 from a writer without a name. I requested a bonus for John, but Hitchcock glowered at me.

"Sonny," he said, "that's the price of admission to the movies."

Months later, Hitch approached me with an offer of $1,500 per week for John's writing services on *To Catch a Thief*. I responded that I wanted $100,000, plus a bonus of $50,000 if no other writer received a credit on the movie. Hitch went crazy and called Lew to complain about me. For a moment I thought I was toast, but Lew backed me up, and Hitch paid. Then came *The Trouble with Harry*. I asked for $250,000, and Hitch coughed it up. Just like that, a star writer was born. John Michael Hayes racked up two Oscar nominations and a mountain of money throughout his career. The truth is, Alfred Hitchcock couldn't tolerate the writing of anyone but my guy. I had the leverage, and it was my job to take advantage of the circumstance.

Everything's a bad idea until it works.

If an idea was obviously smart, then everyone would jump on it without debate. From my experience, the best ideas—or at least the ones that allow you to make a name for yourself—are the least flashy ones. The studio heads in their ivory towers can make splashy peacock deals, but the grinders at the bottom need to make something out of a crow or a sparrow.

This involves you hedging the risk of ridicule within your company, which is a small price to pay when you have a big upside. What would have happened if John Michael Hayes's draft of *Rear Window* was a stinker? Hitchcock would have screamed at the agency—at me in particular—before taking another spin on the roulette wheel of writers. Hayes wouldn't have been to blame for shanking the script, as Hitchcock had a reputation for being a fire-breathing dragon. No one would have gotten fired, and no one's career would have been destroyed. To that effect, I had nothing to lose and everything to gain.

I think this lesson translates to any working environment that exerts a top-down pressure upon employees to perform. Every young caveman is looking to kill a wild boar for the tribe. Don't be afraid to use a net instead of a spear.

As I built my connections and honed my skills as an agent, I was given partial responsibility for handling Revue Studios, MCA's television production company. Our number-one show was *Wagon Train*, which followed a group of frontiersmen trekking from Missouri to California after the Civil War. Starring Ward Bond, the show was broadcast on NBC during prime time. ABC, the caboose of the television distributors, couldn't find a piece of programming to compete with *Wagon Train*. Leonard Goldenson, the president of ABC, had a simple philosophy: "If you can't beat it, buy it." So he waged a battle against NBC from which Revue Studios stood to benefit.

Unbeknownst to NBC, Leonard made me a more than generous offer to take the show to his network. Money and content speaks for itself—I took the figures to Robert Kintner, the president of NBC, and gave him the opportunity to beat the competing bid. As expected, I summoned a hurricane of threats and ill will, but I didn't hear a single sound argument for keeping the show at NBC. I firmed up the deal with ABC, and the show was lifted to the new network. NBC vowed to sever business with MCA as a whole, but we knew they were bluffing. Distributors relied on us for content; without the agency, they were nothing more than pencil pushers with worthless cash. Three months later we sold *The Virginian* to NBC, which replaced *Wagon Train* during prime time. It became readily apparent that content supersedes hate and anger. At the end of the day, if you can provide high-caliber creative material, executives will nuzzle oats out of your hand, no matter how mean they pretend to be.

After eight years at the agency, my career was in fast-forward. At MCA, I stood at the nerve center of the entertainment industry with a hand in each corner of the business. I had an unlimited expense account, a strong client roster, and a trusted mentor who cared about my future. But the dollars didn't reflect my success. I was receiving a modest monthly salary and living off a bonus check given to me each holiday season. I was never certain what the bonus would be, and there was no room negotiating for a larger check. Come December, I'd thank the treasurer before glancing at the check he dropped on my desk, lest I ruffle his feathers. Lew told me repeatedly to remain patient, but Carole was pregnant with Steve, our firstborn, and I had my sights on earning a fortune for the family.

As my concerns at MCA brewed, I received a call from Mark Goodson, the same man who had scorched me years earlier by backing out of the Goodson Todman acquisition. Mark asked whether I'd be interested in jumping ship and trying my hand producing game shows. As vice president of television at MCA, I was making $750 per week; Mark proposed a five-year contract at $2,000 per week, plus 5 percent of profits from all future shows. I'm glad he wasn't in the room with me, because my jaw dropped. My mind raced to leveraging a raise from MCA that matched the proposal.

Although it was fair business, the money-mongering conversation with Lew pained me. He had rolled the dice on me when I had to take out a loan on my suits. When I told Lew the figures, he shook his head.

"That's more money than the head of motion pictures makes," Lew said. Then he opened his drawer, took out a leather folder, and placed it flat on the desk before me.

"Do you know what's in here?" he asked. I shook my head no. "It's the name of the future president of MCA. Your name."

Make a timeline for your inheritance before making a move.

I have to admit, Lew's leather folder move was persuasive. It hit me on a number of levels—to start, MCA was a storied institution in those days. Running the agency would have granted me access to all sectors of the entertainment industry—television, books, motion pictures, music, you name it. On a personal level, I was honored that my mentor viewed me as the future of the company. But as I sat with the decision over a week of sleepless nights, I couldn't deny the undeniable truth. Lew's only way out of MCA was in a body bag. He was never going to retire, which meant I would always stand beneath him. As much as I loved working at MCA, I needed a shot at the steering wheel after eight years of servicing the agency. That meant dissolving my client list and accepting the Goodson Todman offer. No longer would I have twenty-five associates with whom I could socialize and collaborate; I would be the company's sole executive in Los Angeles. For what it's worth, I was right about Lew—he lasted thirty more years running MCA. He and I remained fast friends until his death—we had a standing monthly lunch on our calendars.

It's easy to get romanced by your superiors—especially once you've built a friendship with them. But you can't make it to the top without a clear path to climb. As difficult as it is, sometimes your mentors become your biggest obstacles.

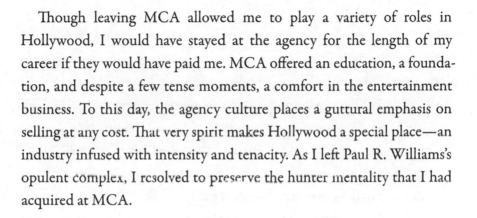

Though leaving MCA allowed me to play a variety of roles in Hollywood, I would have stayed at the agency for the length of my career if they would have paid me. MCA offered an education, a foundation, and despite a few tense moments, a comfort in the entertainment business. To this day, the agency culture places a guttural emphasis on selling at any cost. That very spirit makes Hollywood a special place—an industry infused with intensity and tenacity. As I left Paul R. Williams's opulent complex, I resolved to preserve the hunter mentality that I had acquired at MCA.

A Different Type of Katleman

As long as your nose met the grindstone, vocation didn't matter in the Katleman family. You could be a legal secretary like my mother, a parking lot operator like my father, or a Hollywood agent like me. My uncle Jake and cousin Beldon chose an industry that capitalized on the vices of others: gambling. But they did it with a twist. Jake and Beldon didn't appeal to middle America looking to hit the Powerball; they targeted Hollywood. Their careers showed what happens when you toss entertainment executives into dark casino cellars. You get fireworks.

Jake made his debut in the gambling business as a parking attendant at the Clover Club, Hollywood's playground to the stars. The club was run by Los Angeles's preeminent crime boss, Guy McAfee, a former LAPD officer who turned on the justice system and opened a number of brothels and gambling outfits across the city. The Clover Club was his crown jewel—it became Los Angeles's most lucrative underground casino.

Jake couldn't have been more of an outcast, but what he lacked in shame, he made up in charisma. Within a few months, he had acquired a Rolodex of Hollywood talent including Betty Grable and Humphrey Bogart. Taking careful note of what celebrities loved and hated, he dreamed of creating his own social hub that would attract Hollywood's biggest stars.

Jake built his Eden in Palm Springs and called it The Cove. It was an illegal gambling club that offered booze, live performances, and Humphrey Bogart's favorite chili, cooked by the benevolent Mr. and Mrs. Factor. With gambling outlawed in the state of California, Jake took all the necessary precautions before getting the tables up and running. He paid a handsome bribe to Buron Fitts, the Los Angeles district attorney, to ensure that state troopers wouldn't hamper business. He also installed pillboxes along the club's driveway and hired rifle-bearing guards to protect the high-level visitors inside.

The Cove became every star's forbidden summer camp, where anything could happen. Though Jake was turning major profits, he wanted to move to the big leagues. So he used his savings to buy one of the first Las Vegas casinos: the El Rancho. The stars followed him from one desert to the other like hungry chickens. Of course the demise of The Cove left the Factors without a job, so Jake gave them the money to open their own restaurant. To this day, Factor's Famous Deli is open on Pico Boulevard.

When I was fourteen years old, I spent a summer working the El Rancho as a pool boy. Jake set me up in a fancy room, and I got to watch powerful men and stunning women strut through the desert grounds. The El Rancho was the only hotel in Las Vegas to offer private bungalows to stars like Howard Hughes, Clark Gable, and Cary Grant. Especially in the summers, the grounds were swarming with faces that lived on the screen. More, the guests treated me like a prodigal child, because they thought I was Jake's son. They drunkenly tipped me in gambling chips, and when I cashed out I was shocked by how much money correlated to a brightly painted wafer.

But the money and society weren't the only draws to the El Rancho— the women also roped me in. The El Rancho's most successful live show was called The Follies, which starred a French bombshell called Yellowbird. I would watch her every night with my back pressed to the rear wall of the casino. One evening, I summoned the gall to introduce myself. I learned her real name, Shika, and once she learned that I was related to Jake—let's just say that she rounded out my education.

During my high school spring break, I took a few friends up to the El Rancho. When Jake found me shooting craps, he grabbed me by the collar and yanked me into the back room.

"What are you doing here, Butch?" he asked.

"I'm just here for the free food," I replied. He moved his nose toward my own with gravel in his eyes. Then he slipped a twenty-dollar bill into my palm.

"Dinner's on me tonight. If I see you back at the tables, I'll cut your goddamn hands off."

That was the last time I let Jake find me in his casino. I spent the next decade thinking he was too tough to die. But after I got bumped to MCA's vice president of television, he proved me wrong.

"Jake's gone," my father told me over the phone.

". . . what happened?" I asked soberly.

"A priest and four choirboys."

Jake had been driving to the Las Vegas airport when a station wagon filled with mobsters disguised as the clergy slammed into his vehicle. The killers fled the scene, and Jake was left alone, crushed by his car. The mob had finally caught up to him.

The details behind the hit remain a family mystery to this day. Jake's casino put him into business with some seedy men. It could have been the Purple Gang from Detroit, or Lucky Luciano's group running the Sands—who's to say. But with Jake down for the count, the Katlemans needed to appoint an heir to run the El Rancho.

We called an emergency family meeting in Las Vegas. In one of the resort's boardrooms, the Katleman men assembled: my father, Carl, Maurice, my cousin Beldon, and myself. We needed someone who could stare fear in the face and hold ground against unsavory figures.

"Butch," Carl said. "You've been doing well for yourself in Hollywood. You could pick up where Jake left off, recruiting talent to the casino."

I had worked my tail off to climb the ranks of the agency, and for the first time in my life I felt that I had something to lose. Put simply, I didn't want to tangle with squabbling gangsters.

"Jake told me as a kid that if he ever saw me gambling at the El Rancho, he'd cut my hands off," I said. "I think I better respect his wishes." The room went still before I piped up again.

"Beldon's the man for the job."

And so it was decided—Beldon would take over the El Rancho, and I would return to Beverly Hills.

Different fathers, different results.

I left Las Vegas without knowing what Beldon Katleman was capable of. The following years, however, would demonstrate his genius, as he drastically transformed Jake's watering hole into a gem of the Las Vegas Strip. It would also illuminate that he was a proper crook—the type who could manipulate people into thanking him for ripping them off. I suppose our differences make sense when you consider the men who raised us. While Uncle Maurice was a gangster through and through, my father was a gentleman who wasn't cut out for a life of criminal activities. But putting morality aside, Beldon was a thrill to be around. As he and I rose in our fields, we became like brothers.

Before his Las Vegas days, Beldon was the first of Leonore Annenberg's trio of heavy-hitting husbands. When Beldon proved too difficult to live with, Leonore married Lewis Rosensteil, the multimillionaire founder of the Schenley liquor company, and later Walter Annenberg, the billionaire ex ambassador to the United Kingdom. With respect to honor, I think it's safe to say she failed upward.

Leonore's uncle was Harry Cohn, who ran Columbia Pictures like a fiefdom in the golden age of the studio system. While watching rough cuts, Harry determined whether or not his films needed to be edited by noting if his ass started to ache. Young Beldon capitalized upon his connection to Columbia, and Harry hired him to work on the lot. I have no idea what he did, but knowing Beldon and the flavor of the times, it probably involved some shady behavior.

When World War II hit, Beldon forged a plot to squirm his way out of the draft. All males between the ages of twenty-one and forty-five were forced to register, but Beldon wasn't keen on fighting the Germans. Somehow, he nosed his way into what was called the First Motion Picture Unit. This division of the army was responsible for making training films for soldiers, and they were stationed at Camp Hal Roach, a supposed barracks on a studio lot. Beldon had beaten the system. Decorated as a second lieutenant in the army (which provided him a glossy pension in his later years), Beldon produced short films in his own city. Every evening, he dined with Leonore while his fellow soldiers slogged through the muck in Germany.

By the time the priest and four choirboys murdered Uncle Jake, Beldon's marriage to Leonore had soured. He didn't care about Columbia or the movie business, but he sure revered a glamorous lifestyle. The El Rancho was his ace in the hole. Spending $750,000 on renovations, Beldon turned the resort into the largest hotel in the state of Nevada. Then he turned his attentions to revolutionizing the way that people dined in hotels. In his view, the age of the three-course meal had passed. Red-boothed galleries created a stuffy atmosphere, and menus didn't offer enough options.

"What do we need waiters for, anyway?" Beldon asked. "What if we spent their salaries on better chefs and better food, and the guests served themselves?"

And so Beldon invented the all-you-can-eat buffet. Guests could eat whatever they wanted at any time during their stay, and the El Rancho's popularity skyrocketed. The innovation changed the landscape of dining experiences in hotels across the country. When you're next vacationing, you can blame $200 breakfast tabs on Beldon Katleman.

There was one more area that Beldon would innovate: live performances. Aiming to book the world's greatest acts, he broke the color barrier. African Americans weren't allowed to stay on the Las Vegas Strip when Beldon inherited the hotel. Beldon scoffed at that unwritten rule. He hired the likes of Eartha Kitt, Sammy Davis Jr., Nat King

Cole, and Lena Horne to perform at his casino, and he offered them his best suites. The El Rancho's live performances blew Beldon's competition out of the water and served as bait for celebrity guests. Paul Newman and Joanne Woodward held their wedding in the El Rancho's ballroom, and Howard Hughes graced the casino every time he visited Las Vegas.

Beldon ran his business successfully, but he was not well loved. He didn't care about the Hollywood hierarchy, and he'd cross anyone without blinking. When the high-ranking Universal Studios executive Rufus LeMaire found himself on a cold streak at the craps table, he headed to his room owing the casino $100,000. The following morning, Rufus sneaked back to Los Angeles without paying his debt. Beldon demanded the money, and Rufus refused to pay.

"That's a mistake, Rufus," Beldon said. But Rufus wouldn't be swayed; he didn't think the principles of debt applied to him.

Beldon knew by happenstance that Rufus was terrified of flying, and his lofty post at Universal sent him trotting across the country every month. When Beldon learned that Rufus traveled via the Super Chief, a high-speed train stationed in Pasadena, he bribed the conductor to stop in Las Vegas. Rufus deboarded in the desert to stretch his legs, only to be greeted by the Las Vegas Police, who tackled him to the ground and slapped cuffs on his wrists. With the state of Nevada taking seventeen cents of the casino's every dollar, the Justice Department had a vested interest in indicting Rufus LeMaire. Beldon visited the ashen-faced executive behind bars at the Las Vegas Police Station.

"Hi, Rufus," he said. "Where's my money?"

"I don't have it," Rufus responded. It turned out that Rufus had a gambling problem, and his finances were stretched paper-thin.

So Beldon lobbed a call in to Rufus's superior at Universal and mandated that if the studio wanted its workhorse back, it needed to wire $100,000 to the El Rancho immediately. Within the hour, Beldon had his money and Rufus was on a train to Chicago without any dignity left.

That wasn't the only time that Beldon bullied people in high places. After I became president of television at MGM, I remember the billionaire mogul Kirk Kerkorian smarting when I confirmed my relation to Beldon Katleman.

"Your cousin doesn't have a soft bone in his body," he told me.

Years prior when Kirk owned World Airways, he had spent New Year's Eve at the El Rancho. Kirk had a $100,000 line of credit, and he kicked off the new year by losing every cent. When Kirk headed to his room, bleary-eyed and defeated, he found that his key no longer worked. The concierge regretted to inform him that Beldon had given his room away.

"What are you talking about?" Kirk asked. "I already paid for the room. And I just coughed up $100,000 to the casino."

"It's Mr. Katleman's policy," responded the concierge, "that if you deplete your line of credit, you no longer have a room with us. We gave it to someone who can play the tables."

That was classic Beldon. He spat on all the rules.

Unfortunately for Beldon and the family, his reign at the El Rancho would not last. One evening, the gangster Johnny Roselli walked into the El Rancho and asked to speak with Beldon personally. Johnny was a powerhouse in the Chicago outfit of the Italian mob, answering to the Los Angeles crime boss Jack Dragna. Roselli knew everyone in the criminal underworld. In fact, the CIA handpicked him to consult on a failed hit against Fidel Castro in the early 1960s. Roselli wore a bleached grin when Beldon came out to greet him.

"Congratulations, Beldon!" he exclaimed. "We're business partners."

"Care to elaborate?"

"From now on, we'll be splitting the El Rancho's profits."

"And what will I be getting in return?" Beldon asked stiffly.

"The right to stay in business," responded Roselli.

Beldon had Johnny Roselli escorted off the premises and went to sleep that night with a pistol beneath his pillow. He didn't wake to an Italian trying to gun him down. Instead, he got a call from the hotel's night manager, who said that the El Rancho had burned to the ground during a performance by Betty Grable and Harry James. The guests evacuated without any death or injury, but the casino was a ruin. Beldon found an anonymous note beneath the front door of his bungalow.

"Don't rebuild—don't come back," it read.

That night, Beldon packed his bags and left Sin City for good. He sold the grounds of the El Rancho to Howard Hughes and bought the house of the famed actor Gary Cooper. His days in Las Vegas were over.

Years later, Beldon's phone rang while he was playing a heated game of gin rummy. He labored up to answer.

"Is that so?" he crooned. "Gee, what a shame."

"Who was that?" I asked once Beldon had hung up.

"They found Johnny Roselli stuffed into a fuel drum in Dumfoundling Bay," Beldon said coolly. "He's dead."

"Was that you?" I asked.

"He shouldn't have burned down my casino."

Don't fuck with gangsters.

Johnny Roselli wasn't short on enemies; he could have been killed by a number of men. It could have been the Cubans in retaliation for his plot against Castro, or another gangster in town. Or it could have been my cousin.

In Los Angeles, Beldon became a boisterous socialite who slept with the entire city. His philandering inspired the wrath of his wife Milli, who packed her bags and filed for divorce as quick as her attorney could draw up the paperwork. With Milli out of his life, Beldon began dating the aspiring actress Jackie Lane. I thought that Jackie could be Hollywood's next big star. She had it all: charm, grace, and heart-wrenching looks. There was only one problem: she couldn't act. In fact, she was painful to watch in the audition room.

"Throw her in one of your TV shows, cuz," Beldon begged of me. I was the president of MGM television by then. "It'd mean the world to her." But Jackie turned every line stale, and my producers wouldn't cast her in anything.

Beldon and Jackie's favorite spot in Los Angeles was the Daisy, a star-studded nightclub on Rodeo Drive. As the first members-only discotheque, it attracted figures like Dean Martin and Frank Sinatra. After meeting Beldon and Jackie there on a Saturday night, the gangster Sugar Brown waltzed in. Sugar wasn't someone you wanted to piss off—especially if you had Beldon's less-than-rosy history with the mob. But when he made a move on Jackie, Beldon saw red.

"I'm gonna knock that prick's teeth in," he said through gritted teeth. For some reason, Beldon thought he was a prizefighter of sorts, though he'd never thrown a punch in his life.

Beldon gave Sugar a shove and asked if he wanted to be dragged out of the club in a body bag. Trying to protect my cousin from getting shanked, I darted in between the two men. Next thing I knew, I was on the floor.

Sugar had thrown a right hook intended for Beldon, and his fist connected with my temple. By the time I wobbled back to my feet, the club's owner, Jack Hanson, had tossed Sugar Brown and his cronies onto the curb, and Beldon and Jackie were laughing like hyenas.

"Don't say I'd never take a punch for you," I told my cousin.

Beldon and Jackie had a good time carousing Los Angeles's clubs, but after a while she wanted to settle down. But Jackie wasn't Jewish, and Beldon couldn't bring himself to marry outside the tribe. She ended up giving him the old-fashioned ultimatum: a wedding date or an empty bed. Beldon called Jackie's bluff, and she packed her bags, leaving him with her two afghan hounds.

Now I'm a dog lover, but Jackie's dogs were terrors. I can describe them in three words: big, hairy, and stupid. They used to walk straight through Beldon's screen doors without blinking, and their shedding made it look like Beldon was sleeping with Rapunzel. But Beldon remained adamant on keeping them. He figured Jackie was using them as an excuse to return to Beldon once she cooled off. Within the next few months, Beldon's phone rang. Jackie's voice was on the other end.

"What have you been up to, hon?" he asked, figuring that he'd played his hand perfectly.

"I'm engaged," she said.

". . . to who?"

"You don't know him."

"I know everyone," Beldon said. "Who is he?"

"Prince Alfonso of Hohenlohe."

More accurately, Jackie was engaged to Prince Alfonso Maximiliano Victorio Eugenio Alexandro María Pablo de la Santísima Trinidad y Todos los Santos zu Hohenlohe-Langenburg. The prince could trace his lineage back to the twelfth century, and his ancestors had reigned as princes of the Holy Roman Empire before Napoleon Bonaparte's invasion. Though Prince Alfonso had castles sprinkled all across Europe, his principal residence was in Marbella, Spain. Professionally, he ran and promoted resorts and casinos in Marbella and Costa del Sol. Jackie was engaged to the royal version of Beldon.

I had never seen Beldon in such a state, even after Johnny Roselli incinerated the El Rancho. Maybe Beldon really loved Jackie, or maybe he couldn't stand the fact that he'd been beaten. Whatever the cause, he swore that he would get her back.

"It's the long play, cuz," he told me.

Flash forward three years. Princess Jackie was living with her royal husband in a Spanish castle, with their beautiful baby daughter Arriana sleeping in the world's most expensive crib. Meanwhile, Beldon was still in Los Angeles looking after Jackie's thick-skulled dogs. With spring wilting into summer, the Cannes International Film Festival was just around the corner. I had plans to attend with Kirk Kerkorian, and Beldon decided that he would join us. By this time, Kirk had forgiven Beldon for giving away his hotel room on New Year's Eve.

"Why don't we sail around in Kirk's boat?" Beldon asked. "We'll have a hell of a time."

Kirk agreed, and we flew to Monaco, where Kirk kept his 190-foot yacht. But when we arrived at the dock, we found Beldon holding Jackie's afghans that still didn't know the word *heel*.

"I don't allow cows on board," Kirk grumbled.

"They won't come the whole way—I need to drop them off with Jackie in Marbella. Just a quick pit stop."

Somehow, Kirk didn't object, and we pulled away from the dock.

"What are you planning?" I asked my cousin once we hit the high seas.

"Nothing," he said, smiling. But I had played enough poker with Beldon to tell when he was lying.

Within a few days, we found ourselves approaching the beautiful beaches of Marbella. Waiting for us at the dock was Princess Jackie of Hohenlohe, as radiant as ever. Beldon stood at the bow of Kirk's boat, leashed to the colossal afghans. Kirk and I watched suspiciously as Beldon and Jackie reunited after years of separation.

"Why don't you come aboard for lunch?" Beldon asked her with his million-dollar smile. "I want to hear about this royal life of yours."

Jackie obliged, and Kirk's staff served a meal fit for a princess. Beldon made sure that Jackie had a bottomless supply of wine, constantly tipping the bottle into her crystal-rimmed glass. After a few minutes, the pleasant conversation was drowned out by the clanking of the yacht's anchor. We found ourselves drifting away from the dock.

"Where are we going. . . ?" Jackie said nervously.

"We're taking a cruise around the harbor, hon!"

Beldon was a charmer, but Jackie was no dummy. She realized that she was being kidnapped just before we hit open water.

"What are you doing!" she shrieked.

"Taking you home," Beldon responded. "You should have never married that royal clown."

"I have a daughter! And I'm a princess!"

"We'll hammer out the details later," Beldon said triumphantly.

And so Beldon had plotted to kidnap Jackie Lane in Kirk Kerkorian's yacht. They were like Paris and Helen running off to the city of Troy. But just as Paris didn't consider the wrath of Achilles, Beldon didn't factor in the Spanish Navy. When Prince Alfonso saw our boat breaking away, he dispatched a Spanish destroyer from his armada to sink us and save his damsel. Kirk's yacht was luxurious, but it didn't have the same pick-me-up as a warship. In minutes, we could hear a voice blaring from the Spanish destroyer's speaker.

"*Rendición*! Surrender!"

"Keep going!" Beldon called to the captain.

Next thing I knew, the turret of the destroyer exploded, and a bomb-shell went careening over the mast of our yacht. Now it was time for Kirk, who had been enjoying the spectacle, to take command.

"That's enough," he bellowed. "Turn it around."

"We can beat them!" Beldon yelled.

"I'm not losing my boat because your brain is located at the end of your cock," Kirk responded.

The Spanish Navy raided our boat and extracted the princess and her dogs. To our good fortune, they couldn't indict us because we were over three miles off the coast of Marbella and beyond Spain's internation-al border. Beldon watched Jackie fade into the distance with his heart ripped to shreds. He never spoke to Jackie Lane again, even after she divorced the prince almost a decade later. For the record, she might have made a mistake rejecting Beldon; Jackie received a meager $1 million in her divorce settlement.

"Hardly fit for a princess," she commented on the figure.

If you have the hounds, you have a shot.

Beldon's kidnapping stunt didn't end up working out for him, but his strategy was brilliant. I don't mean to endorse whisking away an ex-be-loved, but rather to identify a key negotiation strategy. From a business sense, it doesn't matter how many times the other side tells you no. If you can retain control over something of value—that is, an object of your opponent's desire—you're still in the game. For Beldon, that was Jackie's afghan hounds, but it could be anything. Go back to Lew Wasserman's sleight of hand in piecing together *Winchester '73*. Bill Goetz needed to cast a major movie star to keep the lights on at Universal, and Lew controlled the career of Jimmy Stewart, Bill's ace in the hole. Lew essentially used Beldon's strategy of kidnapping Jackie to negotiate back-end cash flow for the agency. Go figure.

Beldon didn't stay lonely for long. Back in Los Angeles, he started dating Carol, a former White House intern for John F. Kennedy. Carol had everything Beldon could have asked for: beauty, a sense of humor, and Jewish blood. Before I knew it, I found myself at Beldon and Carol's wedding as my cousin's best man. Beldon had been adamant on the ceremony's location and officiator. It took place at Temple Beth El, the synagogue of the stars, and the union was handled by Rabbi Ott, a close friend of Beldon's. At the reception, I slapped Beldon on the back and joked about how our days of philandering had come to a close.

"Not quite, cuz," he said. Then he sidled up to his bride and cut the cake.

Carol learned within the year that Beldon wasn't cut out for loyalty. He wasn't discreet in his unfaithfulness, either; he consistently staggered home in the early morning hours reeking of the perfume of prostitutes. Carol insisted that they attend couple's therapy, a sanction that Beldon considered worse than hell. But Carol warned that she'd walk out on him, and Beldon didn't have a good track record calling that bluff. The two of them sought a shrink, who refereed their spousal battle. In one of their sessions, the therapist asked Carol to verbalize what she wanted out of Beldon.

"All I want is for him to stop seeing hookers," she declared. "I don't think that's too much to ask of my husband."

"I'm not your husband!" Beldon roared back.

"What are you talking about?" Carol asked.

"The whole wedding was a fake. Why do you think I hired Rabbi Ott? I paid him to muff up the paperwork."

Therein lied Beldon's great secret: his wedding was a sham. While despicable, his deceit was a brilliant financial move. After Carol fled Beldon's house in Beverly Hills for Florida, she quickly found out that he didn't have to pay a cent of alimony. According to the state of California, he had always been a single man.

The clergy has its faults as well.

Member of the tribe or not, Rabbi Ott wasn't immune to Beldon's powers of persuasion. I suppose that all people—even holy men—will break their vows under the right terms.

Beldon returned to his philandering ways without interruption, but I could tell he was missing Carol. After spending a few months with him as a bachelor, I remember his phone erupting from its receiver. I could hear Carol shrieking at the end of the line, but I couldn't make out her words.

"What's the matter, pussycat?" Beldon asked listlessly. A few moments passed. "It wasn't me. Probably suits him right, though." Carol's voice sharpened, and Beldon held the phone away from his ear. "It wasn't me, pussycat," he repeated, and hung up.

"What's the matter?" I asked.

"Oh, nothing. Some sap broke into Carol's house in Florida and shot her new guy through his kneecaps. Her white carpet's ruined."

"It was you, wasn't it?" I said slowly.

"Gotta eliminate the competition."

I don't know how he did it, but within the year Carol had moved back in with Beldon. They were planning a new wedding, where I was Beldon's best man for the second time. This go-round, Carol got to choose the synagogue and the officiator—she decided against Rabbi Ott.

Somehow, Beldon got a happy ending. He lived in Gary Cooper's house for years until Carol found him dead on the tiles of his personal sauna. He had suffered a massive heart attack. Carol still visits his grave at the Hillside Memorial Park in Culver City.

Confidence is everything.

Was Beldon's moral compass askew? Absolutely, but his charm made up for it. He had the vigorous self-assuredness that serves as the secret ingredient in any social landscape. You can convince anyone of anything if you say it with enough volume and repetition. That was Beldon's philosophy, and it sure as hell worked for him.

The Game of Making Game Shows
1962–1970

Mark Goodson and Bill Todman teamed up in the 1940s, well before the advent of the modern game show. Mark was raised cleaning chicken shit on his father's farm in Oakland, California. With watery eyes pinched into a ruddy face, he became a San Francisco radio announcer for a program called *Pop the Question*, which involved contestants lobbing darts at prize-packed balloons. Bill was his opposite—a long-faced, olive-skinned gentleman polished by generations of wealth. He wore dark-framed glasses and spoke with a managerial authority.

Once the duo met in New York, Mark began generating creative radio concepts that Bill sold to broadcasters. They eventually transitioned into television, inventing the quintessential game show. Their first television program, *Winner Take All*, reflected Mark and Bill's business savvy. The episodes were dirt cheap to produce because they didn't require screenwriters or directors. The only real cost involved prizes, which were far less expensive than the million-dollar checks that are necessary for today's programs. When Bill dropped an appliance while walking from his office to the studio, the acclaimed writer Goodman Ace shouted out to him, "Hey, Bill, you dropped your script!"

More, with America burdened by World War II, Mark and Bill could leverage free prizes from manufacturers in exchange for advertising plugs. When the war ended, the company acquired more prizes from overbids at local auctions. They bought in bulk to reduce costs, storing mountains of boats, automobiles, and appliances in a cluttered New York warehouse.

In the early days of the company, Mark and Bill encouraged me to stop by the warehouse and grab a 50-inch television. Unfortunately, I couldn't figure out a way to get the heap of metal back to Los Angeles.

Mark and Bill wanted me to move to their headquarters in New York, but the Big Apple still tasted rotten from my campaign to clean out MCA's East Coast office. My contract made it clear that I would launch Goodson Todman's western operations. Overnight, I had sacrificed the amenities of MCA for four blank walls in the Union Bank office on Wilshire Boulevard. The only asset I brought was my assistant, Janet Quigley. Though I would have never admitted it, I didn't have the slightest clue of what I was doing.

Despite my title of executive vice president, I quickly learned that I'd been hired to fulfill Bill's role in the company. In his prime, Bill Todman was a sales genius with brilliant business acumen. By cutting out the role of writers and directors, he streamlined television and forged a path to modern, non-scripted programming. But by the time I joined the company, Bill had developed a serious drinking problem that laid waste to his perspective. In the mornings he could function at about 70 percent, but around two o'clock he'd begin his daily drink-a-thon. On my first trip to New York after joining the company, I poured myself a glass of water from a carafe in Bill's office, only to find myself gulping lukewarm vodka. Bill's condition reached its peak when he sheared off the side of his Rolls-Royce Corniche on a New York tollbooth. He could barely remember the incident; he just kept on driving into Manhattan without a care in the world. After that episode, Mark and I made sure he had a town car and a driver.

Although the alcohol took Bill out of the game, his presence was invaluable in forcing deals across the goal line. That meant I had to make a number of calls impersonating him, which taught me my next lesson in entertainment. . .

Fake it until you make it.

I spent a good deal of time mimicking Bill's voice and versing myself on the contacts in his Rolodex. I always figured that if I got caught not knowing a key aspect of his life, I would hang up and have Bill blame the episode on temporary amnesia. Luckily, I never had to resort to such a lie, as I made a thick stack of flash cards that noted the personal details of Bill's contacts: spouse names, number of kids, drink preference, etc. I studied harder impersonating Bill Todman than I ever did at UCLA. The whole charade seemed like a joke at the time, but I have to admit: it worked.

As the other face of the company, Mark Goodson was responsible for seeking out material that Bill could sell. He could generate new show concepts and formats like you wouldn't believe. As the company transitioned from radio to television, he prophesized that the radio's successful quiz programs wouldn't translate to the screen because trivia is rewarding to hear, but not to watch. Mark made his shows cinematic and watchable by creating celebrity panels and celebrating the victories of ordinary people. He taught me a lesson that dooms most producers and writers in the business: if you can't summarize a show concept in one sentence, throw it out.

But Mark's creative talents were matched by personal demons. He was one of the most tortured men I met in Hollywood. That's saying a lot in a town that pays $1,000 for a kiss and fifty cents for your soul, according to Marilyn Monroe. With psychiatrists on commission in both New York and Los Angeles, Mark could never be alone, and he always acted like he was broke despite his exorbitant wealth. When I was the president of Fox Television decades later, I invited Mark to fly on the Fox jet with me.

"This is really nice!" he said after takeoff.

"Why don't you buy one?" I asked.

"I can't afford a private jet."

"How much are you worth?"

"... just a shade under $500 million," Mark responded.

"I think that'll do it," I said.

Mark was a man of impeccable taste, with a beautiful suite at 1 Beacon Place, David Rockefeller's building in New York. When the networks started moving to Los Angeles in the 1970s, he bought a suite at the Beverly Hills Hotel, which he refurbished into an exact replica of his New York abode. When it came to women, Mark didn't have much luck. He went through three marriages, all of which ended in messy divorces that left him heartbroken. I could always tell when Mark's love life was in the tubes, because he'd call late-night meetings that required the entire company's attendance. And when he was in between wives or girlfriends, he would force his secretary to drive to his house and read bedtime stories to him. I was reminded of Mark's dependency on women at his funeral where I had to review the company's expenses. I discovered that Mark had been paying a stranger an annual salary of $125,000 for undisclosed services. When I met with the mysterious employee, I gathered that he was Mark's personal pimp, contracted to scout for beautiful women.

"Please don't fire me," he said when I told him his services were no longer needed. "I can find girls for you!" I assured him that I didn't need his help.

By the time I entered the company, Mark and Bill were at each other's throats. Both men had achieved success, and both men had deep insecurities, which presented a dangerous combination. Mark treated Bill with utter disdain, and Bill sought out every opportunity for revenge. Each man's sprawling office—identically sized—was connected by a shared bathroom. Bill would lock Mark's door from the inside of the bathroom, forcing Mark to walk through his own office to use the facilities. From the very onset, I took on the role of peacemaker, trying to hold together a fractured partnership.

Money can't buy self-esteem.

Before I started working with Mark and Bill, I figured the über-wealthy must wake up feeling pretty good about themselves. It didn't take long to learn that members of the top thousandth percent are subject to the same insecurities that cripple adolescent children. It doesn't matter how much money you have going stale in the bank: wealth doesn't cure a pair of head cases.

Under the wing of Mark and Bill, I learned the unique process of game show development. Rather than creating a package and shooting a pilot, networks would base their purchases off a run-through. These were untaped shows with the host and sample contestants, performed for a panel of executives sitting in the front row of an otherwise empty sound stage. It took weeks to get a run-through down perfectly; Mark was a Nazi when it came to the props, contestants, and overall look of the show. But run-throughs were still much cheaper to orchestrate than shooting a pilot. We would schedule all three networks in a single day: ABC at 1:00 p.m.; NBC at 2:00 p.m.; and CBS at 3:00 p.m. If the show was good, we had a bidding war going by dinnertime.

With our shows shot live, I was witness to a number of off-screen meltdowns. In my early days at the company, Mark developed a concept for a musical game show called *Spin to Win*. In the jackpot sequence, which Goodson Todman was bound to finance, contestants were tasked to identify songs played backward. With a thirteen-episode order and very little money, Bill and Mark resolved to choose impossibly obscure songs during the jackpot round. That way, they wouldn't have to shell out money they didn't have.

In the first airing, we decided to throw the "Missouri Waltz" at the nerd who had advanced. I defy you if anyone can identify the "Missouri Waltz"... backward. As the song played, Mark, Bill, and I held our breath in the control room, hoping for the guy to fail. The man took a few beats of intense concentration, listening to the perverted notes of the song. Then his face relaxed, and he smiled into the camera.

"That's the 'Missouri Waltz,'" he said brightly.

"Tell him he's wrong!" Bill screamed into the microphone pegged into the host's ear. But there was nothing we could do. Not only did we have to pay the $25,000 jackpot, we had to produce twelve more episodes without any money. From that point, we took great pains to ensure that Albert Einstein wouldn't be able to guess our jackpot tune.

One of our high-performing shows at Goodson Todman was *To Tell the Truth*. Every episode brought three identically dressed contestants onto the stage, each of whom claimed to be the same person. Two were hacks, and one was authentic. After an onslaught of probing questions, a celebrity panel was tasked to suss out which contestant was telling the truth. Five hours before an evening's shoot, I received a panicked phone call from the production executives. One of our actors had unexpectedly dropped out, and they were in a frenzy to fill his place. I was in New York and therefore an eligible replacement.

"I need three hours to prepare," I demanded.

Whom did I have to impersonate, you may ask? Emmett Kelly, the famous circus clown, who had made his living touring with Barnum & Bailey. Though I didn't know the first thing about clowns, I'd made my living off an ability to improvise. I headed to the closest library and started reading up on clown history. In three hours, I was shaking the hand of the real Mr. Kelly before the cameras started rolling.

"You're toast," I told him. After twenty minutes of questioning, three of the four panel members, including Betty White and Tom Poston, voted for yours truly. Though I consider my performance a résumé sweetener, my wife questioned how much I should celebrate my likeness to a professional circus clown.

"How much money do I get?" I asked Mark after the show.

"You really want the cash? It comes out of your development fund."

"Of course I want it. That's hard-earned money."

I took a crisp check for $750 and went straight to the toy store, where I bought a state-of-the-art wooden swing set for my three kids.

Not every challenge could be solved by acting like a clown. At Goodson Todman, I got the idea of launching a quiz show loosely based on Groucho Marx's *You Bet Your Life*. Just as *You Bet Your* Life relied upon a comic genius like Groucho Marx, this concept was a vehicle to bring a star to the television screen. Who better than Don Rickles, the late king of comedy? I managed to ink a deal, and *The Don Rickles Show* was born.

Despite his pugnacious screen presence, Don was one of the most gracious men in Hollywood. I can't say the same for his manager Joe Scandore, who got ahead in business by tricking gullible Hollywood executives into thinking he played an instrumental role in the Italian mob. Well into production, Don started to veer away from the show's format. The true culprits were the core members of the Rat Pack, whom Don had befriended: Frank Sinatra, Dean Martin, and Joey Bishop. They teased him relentlessly for doing a lowbrow quiz show, and it apparently got under his skin. I received a call from Elton Rule, the president of ABC, who claimed that Don had gone way off script. ABC was right to be upset; they had bought a quiz show — not a variety show. Unfortunately, as the executive producer, it was up to me to keep Don on track. That meant wrangling Scandore.

"We don't want to infringe on Don's freedom to fire from the hip," I told Joe in a crisis meeting, "but we have to stay within the boundaries of the genre. This is a quiz show."

"It's a variety show now. I suggest you knuckle under if you know what's good for you."

The other producers were shaking in their boots. They thought I was putting my life on the line by going toe to toe with Scandore. What they didn't realize, however, was that my cousin Beldon ate hacks like Joe Scandore for breakfast.

"I'll handle it, cuz," Beldon assured me over the phone.

That was the last bit of resistance I got from Joe Scandore; he folded like a cheap deck. It always pays to have people in high places.

My tenure at Goodson Todman coincided with the highly publicized quiz-show scandals of the 1950s. In an effort to boost ratings, producers would manufacture artificial scenarios that forced some contestants to take a fall. When one contestant on the show *Twenty-One* blew the whistle, the entire game show business fell into disarray. The United States government even got involved, shutting down Goodson Todman's crooked competitors. The last men standing were me, Mark, and Bill. Free from legal charges, we had an ostensible monopoly over the business with fifty hours of programming on the air each week. But the scandals had shifted tastes away from quiz shows, which led us to embrace celebrity panels in our shows. That meant we no longer had a place for Ted Beard, Goodson Todman's long-standing quiz writer. When Mark called him into his office, Ted was ready for the inevitable news.

"Consider this early retirement," Mark said. "I'm covering your full salary for the rest of your life."

Behind all of his phobias and neuroses, Mark Goodson was the most generous executive I ever encountered. Not that he was short on money; in the years that followed, we put *The Price Is Right*, *What's My Line*, *I've Got a Secret*, *To Tell the Truth*, *Password*, and *Family Feud* on the air. Goodson Todman became more lucrative than all ten of King Midas's fingers.

When *The Price Is Right* became a smash in 1956, we realized that we could rake in exorbitant sums of money if we could secure daytime and evening broadcasts. However, the powers at CBS refused our request. Back then, production companies could renegotiate a show's distribution deal once a certain period had lapsed. So at the behest of my superiors, I fished for interest from other buyers. If Goodson Todman couldn't change CBS's mind, perhaps a competing offer would. Part of me wanted the other networks to express ambivalence toward the show, because stripping *Price* from CBS could potentially decimate our relationship with the network. But at the end of the day, I was obligated to make the best fiscal maneuver for the company.

When NBC voiced interest in the show, I assumed Bill Todman's character and went head to head with Robert Kintner, the president of NBC. Mark and Bill huddled around the receiver as I studied the index card with all of Robert's personal information on it.

"All right, Bill, let's cut through it," Robert said. "What'll convince you to bring *The Price Is Right* to our network?"

"Five daily broadcasts, plus one evening broadcast per week," I responded.

That was an unprecedented amount of airtime back then. But our hard-nosed approach proved fruitful, as NBC agreed to the terms. I gave CBS a chance to match NBC's offer, but the network wouldn't budge.

"I think you're bluffing," the head of business affairs told me.

We proved him wrong. Goodson Todman moved *The Price Is Right* from CBS to NBC, where it continued to thrive and produce a waterfall of profits. And most importantly, we got the increased number of broadcasts that we wanted.

Business was booming, but Mark and Bill noticed after meeting with their tax attorney that they were getting slammed on astronomical tax rates, especially on investment profits. As I'm sure you know all too well, the government demands taxes on every cent made on investments. With Goodson Todman in the highest tax bracket, the fed was shaving off 50 percent of all investment earnings. The loophole, I learned, involved something called capital gains. I won't bore you with tax jargon, but capital gains guarantee a lower tax rate on profits made by investments. Rather than shelling out 50 percent of our gross, declaring a capital gain meant giving a modest 25 percent to the IRS.

Mark and Bill got it into their heads that they could make millions by taking a capital gain on the sale of *What's My Line*. In other words, they wanted to benefit their tax portfolio by selling the rights to the show to CBS. Let it be known that the network had no need to own the rights, as it was already broadcasting the show. We were trying to sell hot air.

When I made the request to Spencer Harrison, the head of business affairs at CBS, he retorted that we needed to discuss the topic with Bill Paley in person. Of all the high-ranking network executives, Bill Paley, the founder of the Columbia Broadcasting System (CBS), was the most imposing. The son of Jewish-Ukrainian immigrants who made their living selling cigars, Paley launched CBS from a fledgling telecommunications company into a cornerstone of the broadcast business. Bill Todman was in no state to show face before Paley, and Mark wasn't a salesman. I was forced to crawl into the lion's den on my own.

I was sweating through my shirt en route to his office—not because he intimidated me, but because I knew how aggressive our stance was. We weren't offering anything that could benefit CBS; the request was simply for the finances of our own company. If I had learned anything, it was that networks don't like to hand out free gifts. It turns out that Mark and Bill shared my trepidation. As I left the office for my meeting with Paley, they grew paranoid that their business maneuver might sever their relationship with CBS. Unbeknownst to me, they were frantically trying to call off the meeting while I drove to Paley's office. But this was the stone age, before the invention of cell phones, and they never reached me.

Bill Paley towered over me as I sat in his office. In actuality, he had a standing desk because of back problems. But I didn't know about Bill Paley's orthopedic health; I thought he stood up to look down upon his office guests.

"Where's Bill Todman?" he asked me.

"Bill's sick. I'm Harris Katleman."

"What do you want, Harris? We've already told you we want to renew your show."

"With all due respect, any network would kill to renew our show. We want you to buy it."

Mark and Bill were in a panic when I got back to the office, but I had the pleasure of telling them that CBS had rolled over like a dog in the sand. I ended up selling the show to CBS for a figure of $3 million, and Goodson Todman got to declare a capital gain. Not only that, I worked into the deal that Mark and Bill would serve as lifetime executive producers on the title. That little detail was worth $50,000 per episode for Mark and Bill. The company collected the same figure decades later when the show returned to the air.

Those who don't ask definitely won't receive.

The "give me more money" conversation is never a comfortable one, especially when you don't have much leverage. But if you want to ink the deals that really put you in the green, you'll have to swing at a few balls outside the strike zone. Despite the awkwardness of moving *The Price Is Right* from CBS to NBC and begging Bill Paley to buy a show that he already controlled, both of these deals had tremendous impact on the finances of Goodson Todman. There's a good chance you'll get spit on during these tense conversations, but who cares? The upside is too significant to pass up.

❋

With a lofty position in the television marketplace, Goodson Todman expanded its business to include all types of media. Namely, Mark and Bill involved me in the purchase of Rhode Island's foremost newspaper, the *Pawtucket Times*. Let it be known that I didn't know a single iota about the publishing business, but I wasn't about to let anyone else know that. I deployed a mind game that I coined "Thrillseekers"—it involved diving into foreign material and seeing how long it took for someone to recognize my inexperience.

When Mark, Bill, and I flew out to Providence in the dead of winter to sign on the dotted line, we were greeted by a boardroom of waspy New Englanders. By the looks on their faces, they thought us Jews had horns. But we managed to close all the deal points, and afterward we braved the snowstorm to have a drink at the Providence Athletic Club. As they entered, the businessmen handed their topcoats to an African American bellboy. I was the last to step through the revolving door, and I handed the kid a $10 bill: $1 a coat. One of the wasps snatched the bill from the kid and stuffed it into my mitten.

"We only tip ten cents a coat," he said bitterly and handed the kid a dollar.

The purchase of the *Pawtucket Times* got me thinking about other forms of broadcasting that could expand Goodson Todman's brand. On the golf course, I started rubbing elbows with the head of KNBC, Robert Friendly, who indicated that the Seattle radio station KOL was for sale. He argued that radio was more lucrative and less risky than television because it didn't require financing for casting and production. Friendly's pitch seduced me, and I got clearance to buy the station for $1 million. I had immediate buyer's remorse. On my first trip to Seattle, I learned that the station played garbage. This was the early 1960s, when Beatlemania was enrapturing American youths, and KOL played ballads that could lull the Tasmanian Devil to sleep. When I told Mark and Bill that we'd have to rebrand the station, they threw up their hands.

"You bought it. You make it work," Bill said.

I restructured the station in two steps. First, I obtained licensing for pop music that appealed to a younger audience, and second, I hired students at the University of Washington to be disc jockeys. They were dirt cheap to employ, and they appealed to a cooler, younger audience. Thus began the station's arduous climb up Seattle's radio market. We had one major hiccup: the payola scandals. On one of my trips to Seattle, I noticed that my once-ragged college DJs were driving Corvettes. As it turned out, music managers were sending bribes to play their clients' songs on the radio. I had to fire the whole lot of college students to prevent a lawsuit.

After three years, KOL had become the number-one station in the greater Seattle area. I sold the station for far more than we paid for it, which allowed me to center my attentions on what I really cared about: Goodson Todman's scripted television division. After all, I had aspirations beyond producing game shows. Over the years to follow, I shepherded a number of programs through production, including *The Rebel* (1959), *Branded* (1965), *Philip Marlowe* (1959), and *The Richard Boone Show* (1963).

Make your platform work for you.

If you want to produce scripted television, you need some help. You have to accept the collaborative nature of the business, which largely means you can't accomplish much on an island. That means using your company's resources to fuel personal ambitions.

Working out of a nonscripted production company, I lacked a slate of programming, creative support, and recognition from television agents and distributors across town. On the contrary, I controlled a fund from which I could finance and develop projects. Even though Goodson Todman's brand didn't match what I wanted to accomplish, I was able to chase my proverbial cat by taking advantage of the company's resources.

Trying to produce dramas within a company built to produce game shows had its ups and downs. My first at-bat was a half-hour Western called *The Rebel*, which followed an ex-Confederate soldier called

Johnny Yuma. I wanted to do a spectacle show—something that felt both dramatic and adventurous. The writer Andrew J. Fenady wrote a bang-up pilot that attracted the likes of Nick Adams, who had just starred in *Rebel Without a Cause* alongside James Dean. Fenady also inspired the director Irvin Kershner to attach himself, as they had collaborated on a talk show called *Confidential File*. Irvin, who later went on to helm *Star Wars: The Empire Strikes Back*, was an auteur director who popularized the use of the first-person perspective. With Andy, Nick, and Irvin in place, we had ourselves a grade-A package. But Goodson Todman had a reputation as a game show production company, and none of the networks would finance our pilot. That meant we had to front the money ourselves. Mark and Bill gave me a budget of $50,000 and not a cent more. So with a shoestring production, we went into the woodlands beyond Hollywood to shoot.

There's nothing more satisfying than actually liking the first cut of a pilot you've put together. Nick Adams breathed life into Andy's script, and Irvin made the show fun and action packed. There was just one missing element: a theme song.

Find the right jingle.

During my early days at Goodson Todman, Bill told me that every entertainment program needs to get people's feet tapping. He was absolutely right—musical elements play a huge part in capturing an audience. If you don't believe me, try humming the scores of the most successful franchises in movie history: *Star Wars, Harry Potter, Indiana Jones, James Bond, The Lord of the Rings*—the list goes on and on. While television shows lack the budget to bankroll a movie score, the influence of music is still an active force. Think about the theme song for *Friends* or the bass solos that underscore *Seinfeld*. Catching the public's ear is a first step toward catching their eye.

With Bill's advice in mind, Andy and Nick teamed up to write a theme song for *The Rebel*. I have to admit that I wasn't blown away by the first verse:

Johnny Yuma was a rebel,
He wandered through the West
Did Johnny Yuma, the rebel,
He wandered alone.

Not the most inventive lyrics I had ever heard, but I couldn't do any better. Now it was time to find a singer. Later that week, I sat in a conference room opposite a country singer called Johnny Cash. This was before he fell into the haze of his drug habit, and I remember him looking eager and bright-eyed. Unfortunately, I'd already burned through my $50,000 budget, and my superiors had locked up the safe.

"I think you're great," I told Johnny, "but I can't pay you. Will you do it for royalties?"

Johnny and I shook hands, and off he went to record our jingle. Meanwhile, I drove a bidding war between NBC and ABC to finance the full season. I closed with ABC, as they offered to air the show at 9:00 p.m. on Sundays. The development executives at ABC had two major notes for the show, both of which I squashed. First, in an effort to make the show lighter, they wanted to incorporate a dog for Johnny Yuma to talk to. It made no sense. The character had just gotten out of the Civil War—why would he have a dog trotting beside him? The second critique involved our theme song. The executives told us that the singer was off-key. I told them to look up the name of the artist, and we started shooting the rest of the season.

The Rebel became an instant hit with both the critics and the American public. In fact, it was a bit too successful for my old friend Lew Wasserman. When the show debuted in prime time—Sunday evenings at 9:00 p.m.—the number one show was *General Electric Theater*, which was hosted by none other than Wasserman's client Ronald Reagan. Our tiny production company was pitted against the hulking power of

MCA, Revue Studios, and the nation's biggest star. But in just ten weeks, we toppled *General Electric Theater* from its post at the top of the food chain. When Reagan won the presidential election years later, he lobbed an unexpected call into my office.

"Harris—you have partial responsibility for my becoming president."

"How's that?" I asked.

"If it wasn't for Johnny Yuma," he mused, "I'd probably still be hosting that anthology series."

As an unnecessary thank-you, Reagan invited me to his inauguration, though I missed out on a seat in his cabinet. But he and I always remained friendly.

"When this gig is over," I remember him telling me, "find me a show to star in."

Once *The Rebel* got renewed for a second season, Mark and Bill called me the president of Goodson Todman's lost film division and gave me free rein to develop more dramas.

In the years to follow, I developed the scripted series *Philip Marlowe* and *Branded*, but my most ambitious attempt was *The Richard Boone Show*. I had set my eyes upon finding business with the star Richard Boone during my MCA days, romancing his agent Milt Grossman at countless Dodger games. But Milt remained adamant; Richard didn't want to do television.

"He wants to make art with people like Clifford Odets. None of that television crap." Of course, Clifford Odets, one of the foremost playwrights of the time.

"What if I could get Clifford to write for the television screen?" I asked Milt.

"Then it's a different conversation."

I set a meeting with Richard Boone and Clifford Odets, to mixed results. The good news was that they hit it off and wanted to work together. But the erudite Clifford Odets and the pretentious Richard Boone proposed an unsellable format: a repertory series. Rather than a regular series with recurring characters or an anthology series that offered season-long story arcs, Boone and Odets wanted to create stand-alone episodes, much like *The Twilight Zone*. Their program would attract a recurring cast that took on new characters each episode. The goal was to amplify playhouse art into the commercial space of broadcast television.

Over the months to follow, I pieced together a repertory series starring and hosted by Richard Boone, with Clifford Odets writing and executive producing. With respect to creative material, we had zilch. No pilot, no pitch document, no storyline. The plan was to reflect "the manner and morals of contemporary America" through a number of unwritten teleplays. The vague format posed a challenge to my sales abilities—a challenge that I readily accepted. With the package assembled, I needed to find a buyer.

In that economic climate, large corporations bought time slots from the networks. The largest players were Kraft, Philco, Reynolds Metal, and General Electric. Although the broadcasters—ABC, CBS, and NBC—had final approval over content, the corporations financed production and determined what would air. As Reynolds Metal owned NBC's best time slot, I found myself boarding a plane destined for the metal company's headquarters in Richmond, Virginia. NBC had narrowed the competition down to *The Richard Boone Show* and a series from Four Star Productions, a major producer with acclaimed dramas on the air. Reynolds Metals would choose which show aired.

Four Star offered ten executives in the room and a proven track record in scripted programming. I showed up with no one but Richard Boone, which was risky, as he was piss-drunk half of the time. Mark and Bill thought I was spitting into the wind trying to beat Four Star and refused to join. But Boone and I had our pitch down, and somehow we won the time slot. NBC granted us a twenty-five-episode order without a pilot. In the writers' room, we created art-house television—stories that exhibited quality execution and emotional resonance. You can imagine my panic when Clifford Odets dropped dead of stomach cancer five weeks before the series premiere. Matters worsened when Richard Boone got into a serious car accident four weeks later, which required three hundred glass shards to be surgically removed from his eye. The story went down in the tabloids as an accident, but in actuality Richard crashed his Ferrari into a tree while driving drunk. In the passenger seat was Laura Devon, the co-star he was fucking. With both actors married, Laura fled the scene to prevent a full-blown scandal.

Despite the writers' room falling into a spell of chaos, the show received multiple Emmy nominations and a Golden Globe award. Though we were a hit with the critics, let's just say that the show didn't appeal to middle America. *The Richard Boone Show* offered real drama instead of sequin-dressed women dangling prizes before the camera. For the first time, Goodson Todman had produced a prestige project. The show's biggest fan was Mark Goodson, who had finally earned kudos among the echelons of New York's high society. For years, the blue bloods had looked down their noses at Mark for producing game shows, but now he was the real deal.

Just as he made the show great, Richard Boone was responsible for killing it. David Reynolds, who was apparently a massive fan of Boone, asked to take him out to dinner after the first season wrapped. Richard's response to his show's distributor was less than appropriate.

"Tell him to fuck off—he doesn't get to meet the talent."

Reynolds promptly called Mort Werner, the standing chief of NBC, to pull the plug.

"The show's great, but the star's an asshole."

No one could argue with him. In the end, the show's demise was a function of competing egos. There's nothing worse than watching a project you've packaged from scratch die on the vine. But as a salesman, I didn't have control over renewals or cancellations. *The Richard Boone Show* demonstrated that entertainment is all about compromise. You can't expect something as artsy as a repertory series to excel in the ratings.

Conversely, you can't expect garbage content to bode well with the critics. Successful programming toes a very fine line between quality and commerciality.

Think about your tombstone inscription.

The cancellation of *The Richard Boone Show* spurred me to reflect on my career as a whole. After twelve years at Goodson Todman, I'd worked on some of the world's most successful game shows, expanded into newspapers and radio, developed premiere dramatic television, and made a few bucks in the process. But as much as I'd enjoyed myself, I didn't want my tombstone to read, "Here Lies Harris Katleman: Game Show Producer." It was time to make a change.

As gut-wrenching as it is in the moment, failure allows for flashes of clarity. If *The Richard Boone Show* had trucked along for another season or two, I probably would have stayed at Goodson Todman indefinitely and never properly pursued my real goals. When it comes to your dreams, you never want to lose a sense of practicality. That being said, take the time to ask yourself big-picture questions and don't be afraid to call an audible. Otherwise, you're bound to fall short of your ambitions.

A Casino Man's Big Gamble
1972–1977

As my unhappiness at Goodson Todman marinated, I received an offer from Four Star Productions, the same company that I beat out with *The Richard Boone Show*. Spawned by a foursome of classic actors—Dick Powell, David Niven, Charles Boyer, and Ida Lupino—the company produced highbrow television content. The company was in the hands of David Charnay, a PR man from Manhattan. I didn't know Charnay personally, but I liked the sound of benefiting from the Four Star banner. I agreed to jump ship on the condition that I would be running television with complete autonomy.

Working at Four Star Productions turned out to be a disaster. I recognized red flag number one when Charnay tried casting his bimbo girlfriend in our shows. Within six months, he had made a number of horrendous deals behind my back. One Monday morning, he revealed he had signed the defunct actor Anthony Quinn.

"Anthony Quinn is over the hill," I told Charnay, but he insisted that he could raise the company to new heights. I thought that was my job. More, I learned upon milling through the books that the company didn't have the capital to launch top-level television programs, let alone movies, as Charnay had assured. I'd learned to never compound an initial mistake with another mistake—it's always better to swallow your pride and cut your losses.

Leap off the boat before it goes under.

There's a key difference between quitting and self-preservation. You never want to preemptively give up on a challenging situation, but you also don't want to get caught in a dumpster fire. When I slipped out of my contract with Four Star Productions, I lacked a tangible foothold in Hollywood. Unlike my transitions between MCA, Goodson Todman, and Four Star, I didn't have a competing offer from another entertainment outfit. Mark Goodson and Bill Todman lobbied for my return to the game show business, but I had learned my lesson to wait for the right gig. Hell-bent on developing scripted content, I decided to be patient for the right position to open up.

Your reputation is all you have. Better to be unemployed than married to a failing company.

During my hiatus, I consulted for a few podunk production companies, including Cinemation Industries. They produced exploitation films—movies that capitalized upon the shock value of lurid content. Their most successful production was *Fritz the Cat*, an X-rated cartoon brimming with political satire, drug binges, and orgy scenes. Anyone naive enough to think the public reveres good storytelling should watch *Fritz*; the film grossed $90 million off a $850,000 budget. A couple months working with Jerry Gross, the head of Cinemation, confirmed that developing bad scripts is worse than developing no scripts. I made the right move leaving; the company went bankrupt and Jerry ended up taking a job at 7-Eleven.

Though I didn't have a secure job, I still had my connections. About a year after I left Four Star, the powerhouse attorney Greg Bautzer asked me to meet him for lunch. Greg was one of Hollywood's brightest executives, representing stars like Ingrid Bergman, Frank Sinatra, and Howard Hughes. Blessed with undeniable charisma and good looks, people used to wonder why Greg wasn't talent. He would have answered that actors don't wield enough power over the business.

We met at the Bistro, the industry's eminent watering hole for A-listers. Years prior, Beldon had convinced me to put up $5,000 for an interest in one of the restaurant booths—the investment all but guaranteed a reservation. Coughing up that cash was one of the best moves I made as a young executive; the other investors included Jack Benny, Dean Martin, and Sammy Davis Jr.

Greg told me that his client Kirk Kerkorian, the owner of MGM, wanted to meet with me in Palm Springs.

"What does Kirk want from me?" I asked.

"Just go sit with him," he responded lackadaisically. "See if you guys hit it off."

The youngest of four, Kerkor Kerkorian was born to Armenian farmers in Fresno, the navel of California. He grew up with zilch—his parents had taken out lead-clad mortgages on a number of farms that all failed, and the Kerkorians owed money all over the Central Valley. Kirk was thrust into real estate at the age of four when Mr. Kerkorian maxed out his credit limit and took out a loan under his son's name. The farm fell into a tailspin in the early 1920s, and the Kerkorians were forced to move into South Los Angeles, uprooting every few months to avoid rent collectors. Speaking only Armenian, Kirk learned English as a second language but had to drop out of school in the eighth grade to support his family. His farming skill set didn't exactly translate to urban disciplines, so Kirk took up boxing. He toggled through a number of nicknames, including the Bakersfield Bomber and Rifle Right Kerkorian throughout his career of thirty-three wins, four losses, and a Pacific welterweight title.

During his side job installing furnaces, Kirk befriended an amateur pilot who offered to take him on a ride-along in his single-engine aircraft. From the moment they left the runway, Kirk was transfixed by the world of flight. He moved to the Mojave Desert to study at the Happy Bottom Riding Club, every aviator's favorite spot in Southern California. The establishment was run by the famous aviatrix Florence "Pancho" Barnes, who founded the first union for stunt pilots. The desert proved to be a place suited to Kirk's strengths; he offered to milk Pancho's cattle and scoop manure in exchange for flying lessons. As World War II intensified, Kirk obtained his pilot's license and got a job ferrying fighter jets from Canada to Scotland for the British Royal Air Force. Each trip was fraught with risk—the fighter jets had brittle wings that were subject to icing over in the Arctic Circle and small fuel tanks that could barely sustain a flight across the Atlantic Ocean. On one occasion, Kirk ran out of gas a few miles before the Scotland airstrip and had to glide into the landing zone without any engine power.

With a small wad of cash in his pocket, Kirk made his first investment in a Cessna aircraft. He planned to make his income through two different revenue streams: 1) by offering private flight classes and 2) by providing a private charter service from Los Angeles to Las Vegas. It was 1945, the year that World War II ended, and Las Vegas was still a dark, dry desert pocked with sparse gambling houses. Kirk detected the magic of Sin City before it became the mecca of nightlife. During layovers in Las Vegas, he became a serious craps player. Whether he made a killing or lost a fortune, he gained a reputation for being unflappable. Kirk didn't scowl or glower like the other gamblers at the table; he wore a bemused smile that covered his thoughts and emotions like black on night. His gambling winnings provided the capital to buy the Los Angeles Air Service, which he renamed Trans International Airlines (TIA). Noticing that fuel was in short supply, Kirk made massive profits by draining his planes' tanks and selling the fuel to larger competitors. He made his first million dollars selling the airline and poured every cent into eighty acres of Las Vegas real estate. Three years later, he repurchased TIA and sold the company to the TransAmerica Corporation for $85 million.

As the dominant tycoon in the flight business, Kirk turned his attentions toward developing the mega resort. Throughout his history of hotel acquisitions, Kirk bought the world's largest hotel on three different occasions: first, the International Hotel (now the Westgate Las Vegas), then the MGM Grand Hotel, and finally the MGM Grand. Kirk was the first to create a singular resort destination that met the needs of every guest. His vision of Las Vegas attracted bachelors looking for trouble along with children hankering for waterslides.

In 1969, Kirk indulged his interest in the entertainment industry by prying MGM from its existing stockholders. He flipped the studio conglomerate three times before ending the studio's independent power by selling to the Sony Corporation in 2004. In his final years, Kirk delved into the automobile business by buying and selling stakes in Chrysler and General Motors. The impoverished son of Armenian farmers was worth $16 billion at his peak wealth.

Prior to my lunch with Greg Bautzer, I had never met the legendary mogul. He had a reputation for being a bit of a recluse, known for rejecting invitations to the Academy Awards in protest of Hollywood's culture of excess. I didn't have an inkling as to what awaited me in Palm Springs, but I sure was curious. The next day I found myself at the Santa Monica Airport boarding a private Learjet bound for the desert. A limousine was waiting for me on the tarmac when I arrived. The driver wound through the heart of Palm Springs and rolled into the driveway of Kirk's private home. Kirk greeted me at the front door, wearing a crisp, white shirt and a herringbone blazer. The first thing I noticed was his poker face: his signature bemused smile that veiled excitement and rage alike. He was a true riverboat gambler—absolutely unreadable.

For one of the world's richest men, Kirk had no taste whatsoever. If I hadn't known how much money he had, I would have guessed that he'd furnished his living room with IKEA products. As we sat, Kirk began lamenting the dire state of MGM Television under its current president. The only show on air was *Medical Center*, a tedious boilerplate drama that middle America consumed like slop. To my surprise, Kirk asked me how I would turn the operation around. It slowly dawned upon me; this was more of an interview than a chat. After three hours of conversation, Kirk asked if I wanted to serve as the new president of MGM Television. I couldn't believe it.

"I don't know how to run a studio," I said.

"Neither do I," he responded. "You can't fall off the floor."

You can't fall off the floor.

There are a few instances in a person's career that demand throwing caution to the wind. Speaking frankly, I had no idea how to make the high-stakes decisions of a studio president. Let's review my résumé to date: ice deliveryman, vice president of television at MCA, vice president of production at Goodson Todman, and head of sales at Four Star Productions. We can forget about my stint with the fathers of *Fritz the Cat*. Though I had grown into a seasoned salesman, I was a child wandering in the forest when it came to running a studio. But when the chance to do something great comes along, you can't be afraid to take advantage of it. Looking back, I realize that Kirk didn't want a seasoned veteran for the job—he wanted a fresh outside man who could breathe some life into the television department.

During my first week at MGM, I met with the controller, Les Friends, without a clue as to what he wanted to discuss. He took a seat across my desk and pulled a thick legal pad from his briefcase.

"Have you prepared your projection yet?" he asked me.

"What do you mean?"

"The banks are all living on loans," Les said. "We need to record an estimate of how many shows you'll have on the air next year."

"Oh. Twenty," I said.

"Twenty!" No studio in history had ever held that much programming.

"I won't be here in five years," I said with a shrug. I suppose I hadn't shaken Lew Wasserman's tendency to make promises first and figure out the details later.

The routine of a studio president was like nothing I had ever experienced. My daily mood was determined by a call at 6:00 a.m. with the ratings. I quickly learned that reigning over a studio meant enslavement to the public's reception. There's no better feeling than witnessing your show beat its competitors, and no worse defeat than watching the fruits of your labor crumble. I had two primary methods of boosting the ratings. First off, I devoted a significant chunk of my discretionary fund to radio advertising. I couldn't afford commercials on television, but audio campaigns and promotions made a major impact on the public's resolve to tune in. Secondly, I employed my research team to lobby for the best time slots on a network's schedule. If you're looking at the factors that determine a show's success, scheduling is at the very top. You don't want to waste a hit show on Saturday nights when no one's watching, and you can't let a fledgling program get slaughtered during prime time. Broadcasting research gave me hard data that paired the right show with the right time slot.

Aside from numbers, network relationships played a pivotal role in determining airings and renewals. The buyers at the network determined which shows lived and died, so I had to ensure that they liked me better than rival studio presidents. When buyers are faced with renewing one out of two programs, they tend to choose the one backed by the president who provided free lift tickets in Aspen. In addition to the decision makers, I took a special interest in romancing the people who drafted renewal contracts: the business affairs executives at the networks. By treating lawyers like celebrities, I got far more intel on buying trends and series pickups than I ever expected.

It didn't take a high IQ to recognize that if I wanted to run a top-notch studio, I needed to sign top-notch creatives. With my background at MCA, I figured this would be the easiest part of my job. I thought wrong. An insider analysis of MGM's finances revealed that the entire company was teetering on massive loans to fund Kirk's hotels. In other words, we had no money to pay elite creators. To skirt our lack of capital, I recruited writers and producers by offering them executive assistants as well as plush offices on the MGM lot. This way, they got the full studio treatment without me having to pay a cent up front. More, it preserved the illusion that MGM was a heavy hitter among Hollywood's crop of television studios.

Kirk, meanwhile, couldn't have cared less about my strategies running the studio. When I asked him if he wanted to consult on my production slate, he almost laughed at me.

"Just show me the money," he said.

With Kirk's focus on Las Vegas, the super executive Jim Aubrey ran the studio. Coined "The Smiling Cobra," Jim Aubrey was the quintessential self-diagnosed Hollywood villain. A star left end on Princeton's football team, Jim graduated to serve in the air force during World War II. In business, he was a workaholic who achieved his goals through ambiguous moral standards.

Jim had served as the president of CBS after his predecessor Louis Cowan was ousted as a result of the quiz scandals—the same catalyst for my success at Goodson Todman. Harboring fierce contempt for Bill Paley, the CEO of CBS, Aubrey searched for investors to buy the company and depose his boss. He also had shady spending habits, to say the least. Without telling his superiors, he used CBS money to buy Jackie Gleason a futuristic round home in Peekskill, New York. He was later exposed for accepting kickbacks from producers. Martin Ransohoff, who worked with Aubrey on multiple CBS programs, bankrolled an apartment in New York and a late-night chauffeur for his philandering. But Jim's successes eclipsed his sketchiness. Green-lighting smash hits like *The Beverly Hillbillies* and *Gilligan's Island*, he had fourteen of the top fifteen prime-time shows on his network. Jim developed a superficial yet effective filmmaking formula that prevails today: "Broads, Bosoms, and Fun." The powerhouse agent Sue Mengers famously summed up Jim's presence and tough stance on deal making by saying she'd rather go to bed with him than negotiate with him.

Jim just might have been the most hated man in show business, which was saying a lot. Not only was he Hollywood's most prolific womanizer, he had an affinity for beating up women. According to my associate Cecil Barker, who worked beneath Jim as an executive producer on *Streets of San Francisco*, Bill Paley fired Jim for assaulting the woman he was dating: the daughter of a US senator. In a fit of rage, he allegedly flung the poor woman down a flight of stairs. The senator in turn threatened to wage war on CBS if Jim Aubrey wasn't immediately fired, and Bill Paley threw him to the curb without blinking.

Luckily for Jim, his lawyer was the mastermind Greg Bautzer. Just as Greg endorsed me to run MGM Television, he talked Kirk into hiring Jim. If the company was struggling when I entered, it was in utter free fall when Jim took the reins. He made a number of aggressive maneuvers to restore MGM to its former status as a powerhouse among the other studios. First, he moved MGM's headquarters from New York to Culver City with the intent of syncing the studio's financial and production sectors. Good move. Then, he sold the majority of the studio's back lot to developers and investors. Very, very bad move. The term *back lot* is a misnomer—*city* is more appropriate. MGM's original property spanned 187 acres, with thirty-three soundstages, two hundred buildings, and a twelve-million-gallon lake. That land provided dense jungles for *Tarzan*, French countrysides for *The Three Musketeers*, and battlegrounds for *The Four Horsemen of the Apocalypse*. I can only imagine how much that real estate would go for in today's climate.

Jim proceeded to slash budgets and seize creative control of each MGM production, which made filmmakers, producers, and creatives go berserk. In fact, when the MGM film *Chandler* bombed with critics and moviegoers alike, the director Paul Magwood and his producer Michael S. Laughlin spent the money to take out a full page in the trades that carried the following black-bordered message:

"Regarding what was our film *Chandler*, let's give credit where credit is due. We sadly acknowledge that all editing, postproduction, as well as additional scenes were executed by James T. Aubrey Jr. We are sorry."

Perhaps most controversially, Jim effectively liquidated the studio. He had a no-nostalgia policy, selling massive portions of studio assets to fund Kirk's hospitality business. That included Dorothy's ruby slippers from *The Wizard of Oz*.

Hollywood doesn't have checks or balances.

Anyone privy to the trenches of the entertainment business knows that the principles of the Constitution don't apply. The industry operates more like an autocracy than anything else. That means an endless cycle of executives' rapid rise to power, punctuated by dramatic falls from grace. With individuals acquiring heaps of power, a single managerial decision can either decimate or bless an entire company. If you want to survive in the entertainment industry, you better be able to handle a revolving door of regime changes.

Despite Jim's controversial tactics, he treated me like a white knight. I never knew why he liked me so much—maybe because we had both played football, maybe because he liked my take-no-prisoners attitude. Whatever the reason, he gave me the freedom to swing freely. That being said, he was a miser when it came to budgeting. A year or so into my position, I hatched a prank that pinched Jim for his stinginess. We were in New York during selling season, and after a successful day of wheeling and dealing, the MGM team met for dinner at PJ Clark's. We had booked a private room in the back of the restaurant and ordered enough food to feed Napoleon's army. Little by little, the executives checked their watches and slipped out of the room, claiming that a buyer wanted to meet for drinks that evening. Finally, the room housed just me, Jim, and a boneyard of picked steaks. Just as Jim cocked his head suspiciously, our waiter alerted me that Kirk Kerkorian was trying to reach me. Before Jim could get a word in, I was out the door grinning. I met the other executives by the front door and headed back to the hotel as the busboy delivered a check for $1,100, which Jim had to cover personally.

With two enigmas for bosses and a failing department, I had to carve a new slate of shows from the ground up. More, the company culture was in the tubes. Walking onto the MGM lot felt more like entering a bullpen of cubicles than a nerve center for storytelling with nearly fifty years of history. I remedied that by acquainting myself with the executives on the lot. During my first week on the job, I passed an office where a man was packing his belongings. Curious, I popped my head in and asked him where he was going.

"Home, I guess. Kirk brought in a foreigner to run MGM Television—I figure I'm next on the chopping block."

I shook the man's hand and introduced myself as Harris Katleman. He looked at me like his eyelids had been cut off.

"What do you do around here?" I asked.

"I run development" was his reply.

"Are you good?"

"Very," he said.

The man's name was Barry Lowen, and he became my most valuable colleague throughout my tenure at MGM. You can have the content, relationships, and reputation, but if you don't have the right workhorses behind you, you're dead in the water. When I left MGM years later, I brought Barry with me to Columbia Pictures. And when I became the president of Twentieth Century Fox Television, I brought him to the Fox lot. My friendship with Barry raised a lot of eyebrows at MGM, on account of Barry's coming out. Kirk had bought a suite at the Carlyle Hotel in New York for senior executives to use on business, and come selling season, I would let Barry sleep in the guest room.

"Not a good look to share a suite with a gay man, Harris," everyone told me, but I didn't care. He was a cornerstone for my success at the studio.

Though I inherited the talents of Barry Lowen by chance, the other members of my team were third-string players with no mojo. I remember stopping in my tracks after entering the office of a business affairs executive who shall remain nameless. He had a loaded revolver sitting on his desk.

"What are you doing with a firearm?" I asked.

"You never know what's gonna happen around here," he responded eerily.

My first thought was to fire him on the spot, but I didn't want to get killed. I decided to bring in someone over him and keep him on payroll. If anything was for certain, I needed to assemble my own team.

Enter Bill Haber, an agent at the William Morris Agency whom I had met during my days at Goodson Todman. With solid relationships in the scripted television business, he introduced me to the executives who would define the success of my career. As I scouted for hires, I wasn't looking to fill a stock number of open positions at MGM. Rather, I wanted to insulate myself with people I could trust for the long haul.

Surrounding myself with development experts took pressure off my inexperience, but at the end of the day, I was responsible for green-lighting programs for MGM. I could sell bottled air if I had to, but I didn't know how to develop. So I resolved to adapt a number of top-grade MGM films for television. That strategy provided for a decent first pilot season—I got two shows on the air: *Adam's Rib* and *The Courtship of Eddie's Father*. We faced a minor production hang up on *Adam's Rib*—our leading lady, Blythe Danner, had just given birth to Gwyneth Paltrow. Baby Gwyneth sat in a cradle on set, and every time she cried, Blythe lactated through her shirt. At first the producers found it funny, but after a few repeated occurrences, it became a major inconvenience for the production. Blythe would have to step out of character to feed Gwyneth, and then she'd need a wardrobe change. It got to the point where my line producer suggested duct-taping the baby's mouth shut. I'd like to think he was joking, but who knows. Stress can cloud one's judgment.

My second year at MGM was a complete and utter bust. Of the seven pilots that we shot and produced, we sold a goose egg.

"Should I pack my bags for Europe?" I asked Kirk in a private meeting.

"Hang in and keep swinging—let's try another year."

The next season, we went four for four, and MGM made a killing. I had finally gotten the hang of running a studio.

Over the years, I maintained a close friendship with Bill Haber. He had a standing invitation to my seats at the Los Angeles Raiders games, and we played in a monthly poker game together. Despite our friendship, we had a few standoffs that we settled with a gamble. Bill represented the famed actor Lou Gossett, whose mile-long CV might be best punctuated by his performance in *Enemy Mine*. I was putting together a TV movie called *The Fuzz Brothers*, and Bill and I were in the heat of negotiations for Lou to star. With a meager production budget, I was playing the miser. I slipped Bill an offer for $5,000, which he laughed at. My figure needed to double according to him.

"I'll tell you what. We'll flip a coin for it. Heads he gets ten grand, tails he gets five."

Bill couldn't resist the temptation of friendly competition and begrudgingly agreed. I won the toss, and Lou Gossett Jr. starred in *The Fuzz Brothers* for half his quote. Though I got lucky the first go-round, Bill got the last laugh. Decades later when I was the president of Twentieth Century Fox, we produced a show that Bill had packaged. When I looked over the books, I realized that we were strapped for cash. I called Bill and told him that I couldn't pay him his 5 percent packaging fee.

"You can't or you won't?" he asked me angrily.

"A mixture of the two" was my response. This time, Bill goaded me into a game of chance.

"Let's settle it over a hand of gin," he said. "If you win, we'll call it 2.5 percent. If I win, I'll take my 5 percent."

With Barry Lowen in the room as a witness, Bill and I sat in my office and played a heated hand of gin rummy. Karma was on his side—his aces beat my kings. Bill got his 5 percent and left my office with a shit-eating grin.

At MGM, I learned that Bill was miserable at his agency. As Hollywood's oldest, most antiquated representation company, the William Morris Agency treated its employees like numbers. In confidence, Bill revealed to me that he and a few trusted colleagues were splintering off to form their own group. That sounded great to me. I liked the idea of having an additional agency where I could shop material—I was in favor of anything that brought more players to the game. A few weeks later, Bill called me on my personal phone line.

"We're fucked," he said. "The higher-ups at William Morris found out about our coup. They kicked us out."

Bill and the four other defectors were renting a cramped office space in the Hong Kong Bank Building. Their wives were acting as their secretaries.

"Why don't you come to the MGM lot until you get your shit together?" I asked. If Bill could have kissed me through the phone line, he would have.

"Two things I have to ask before you move in. . . who are your partners, and what are you naming your business?"

"Rowland Perkins, Ron Meyer, Mike Rosenfeld, and Michael Ovitz," Bill replied. "We're calling it the Creative Artists Agency. CAA."

A few days later, I received a call from Kirk Kerkorian. He had an uncharacteristic stiffness in his voice.

"Harris, come to my house right now."

I knew that couldn't be good—I'd never even been to Kirk's Los Angeles residence. When Kirk answered his door, he was as angry as I'd ever seen him.

"Did you offer office space to that splinter of William Morris?" he asked.
"Sure I did."

Kirk shook his head with disgust. "Sam Weisbord, Abe Lastfogel, and the senior partners found out you're helping the deserters. They're blackballing us—all William Morris clients are banned from doing business with MGM."

I could tell that the next words out of my mouth would determine whether or not I had a future at the company. I chose my words carefully.

"Kirk, do you remember the early days of Trans International Airlines, when you spent your savings on a rusty fleet of World War II bombers?"

Kirk nodded.

"And do you remember when United, American, and TWA tried to run you out of business?"

He nodded again.

"I don't have to tell you that all great things start small. I won't apologize for helping my allies."

"All right, Harris," Kirk said, cocking his head. "Whatever you say."

Help your friends off the canvas.

Helping Bill didn't make me any friends at the William Morris office, but what did I care? They still had to do business with the president of MGM Television. In exchange for a few ruffled feathers, I gained the lifelong support of CAA, which ultimately became the biggest show in town. Today, Bill's fledgling agency handles Hollywood's most prolific actors and actresses and plays a dominant role in every corner of the business. When your colleagues look to be down for the count, you have an opportunity to gain lifelong support and fervent loyalty. All you have to do is help them climb to their feet.

Just over a year into my tenure at MGM, Kirk got fed up with the performance of the movie department, and Jim Aubrey got the ax. Jim had successfully alienated the most respected creatives in the business with his abrasive personality, and the majority of his films had tanked. I remember reviewing the performance of the studio in a room with Kirk and Greg Bautzer. The movie numbers spoke for themselves.

"I guess we have to cut The Smiling Cobra loose," Greg said quietly.

"Yep" was Kirk's response.

"When are you going to tell him?" Greg asked. Greg represented Jim—he had to handle the matter very carefully.

"Greg. . . you hired him, you fire him," Kirk said.

Jim probably deserved it, but I wasn't thrilled with the shakeup. Expecting a studio to succeed through a jumble of leadership changes is like expecting a Super Bowl victory out of a football team that can't lock in a franchise quarterback. Studios need consistency in order to fare well in the marketplace.

In hiring Jim and me, Kirk had a history of selecting unorthodox executives for high-level posts. This time around, Kirk would honor the whiny-voiced Frank Rosenfelt, an attorney from MGM's legal department. I shook my new boss's hand, hoping for the best and expecting the worst. My expectations were met. Frank was a terror who ran the studio solely by the numbers, as if entertainment programming was a math equation. He demonstrated his incompetence by costing MGM millions of dollars with the television series *CHiPs*. Rick Rosner, a young producer, had approached me with a drama concept that tracked the lives of California highway patrolmen, and I had moved the pilot into production. To close Rick's deal, Frank stepped in and gave Rick 50 percent of the show's profits.

"You can't do that," I tried to explain. "If the show's a hit, we'll lose a fortune."

"It's not gonna be a hit," Frank responded.

CHiPs ran for 139 episodes over six seasons. Every time I bump into Rick Rosner around town, he thanks me for his $25 million paycheck. I grumble the same response to him.

"Thank Frank Rosenfelt."

Never underestimate the back end.

In the television business, there are two chief ways of compensating talent: 1) you can pay an up-front fee in exchange for services or 2) you can give away a percentage of the show's profits. For obvious reasons, the first method is far less ambiguous; it's a flat fee that doesn't rely on a show's performance. The second method is a wild card: if a show smashes, back-end shares can create inexhaustible cash streams. If a show bombs, percentages are less valuable than a lump of coal.

When executives are feeling thrifty or nervous about a show's quality, they tend to offer back-end percentages as opposed to up-front fees. This allows them to push a show through the pipeline without dipping into their development funds. But as evidenced in the *CHiPs* case, this strategy can lead to disastrous results. Even the brainiacs of creative accounting couldn't find a way to box Rick Rosner out of his shares. It's important to remember that while shows come and go, a single deal can have lasting effects on a studio.

Though Kirk enjoyed the entertainment industry, his hotel business was always his real priority. And despite his billionaire status, he used my department to curb financial hardships, namely that which accompanied construction on the MGM Grand. Located right on the Las Vegas Strip, Kirk's latest endeavor was to be the largest, most luxurious resort in the United States. With nearly fifty-five hundred rooms and sprawling auditoriums for live entertainment, the MGM Grand was Kirk's version of Disneyland. About halfway through its construction, he lobbed a call in to my office.

"Harris," he said without a wire of tension in his voice, "we're short $90 million in building the hotel. I figured you're the type of guy who thinks off the wall. . . got any ideas?"

I had been largely kept in the dark on matters pertaining to Kirk's hotels, so I figured calling me for advice meant we were in deep trouble. With MGM owning the rights to classic movies like *2001: A Space Odyssey*, *Gone with the Wind*, and *Dr. Zhivago*, I suggested selling MGM's crown jewels. But the bank precluded us from reducing the assets of the company. In other words, we couldn't sell jack. I reflected upon the wisdom of Lew Wasserman: one good contact can solve any problem. In this case, that contact had to be an entity that was more underwater than we were. CBS came to mind—*The Merv Griffin Show* had just gotten slaughtered against *The Johnny Carson Show*, and the network was hemorrhaging money. It didn't have anything to fill a prime-time slot, let alone a piece of programming that could beat Carson. Except, I thought, one of MGM's classic films.

A quick bit of film history: at that period in time, the movie business held an embargo against networks because television threatened the box office. Film executives upheld an unwritten rule to never license movies for television. That way, film audiences were forced to flock to theaters. I figured that I could leverage a sum of $90 million if MGM was the first company to break the standard. With success, we would receive the wrath of film executives and potentially ruin the movie business. But we also stood to make a fortune.

I called Bob Daly, the head of business affairs at CBS, and asked if he'd be interested in licensing MGM movies to CBS late night for television broadcasts. Bob couldn't believe it; he proceeded to run the idea up the CBS flagpole.

"If you're bullshitting me, they'll fire me and I'll kill you," he said. I informed Kirk of my idea, maintaining that we had a strong nibble from CBS. My suspicions were confirmed: the studio was about to implode, and Kirk was willing to take any action to keep the studio afloat.

"We're on the brink of bankruptcy," Kirk said. "Do what you need to do." Within the hour, Bob Daly told me he had the green light from Bill Paley. The plan was a go.

"Here's the caveat," I said. "We need $90 million in seven days."

Bob nearly blew out an artery. MGM would license three hundred films, with a price tag of $30,000 per airing. Each title needed to be legally vetted on an individual basis. I summoned a legal orgy in New York, where the MGM and CBS business affairs departments sat in a room for seven days to finalize the contracts. After consuming countless pots of coffee and deli sandwiches, I held a crisp check for $90 million. I got Kirk on the phone and told him I was coming to Los Angeles with the money.

"Fly straight to Vegas and deposit it at the Bank of Nevada. We need it now."

So I flew to the desert, where I deposited the full amount for Kirk. The money went straight to construction debt for the MGM Grand hotel, and the debacle never even hit the trades. When I finally pulled up to my house in Beverly Hills that night, I found a new 450 SL Mercedes sitting in my driveway. There was a note on the windshield from Kirk Kerkorian.

"Thanks," it read.

That wasn't the only time Kirk used television to finance his entrepreneurial exploits. Though we had nicked the membrane of MGM's library with the $90 million deal, the bank had forced us to hold on to our three biggest titles: *Gone with the Wind*, *Dr. Zhivago*, and *2001: A Space Odyssey*. But once Kirk finished building the MGM Grand, he was free to profit off the classics by selling them to networks. Having calculated the colossal licensing fees he could turn, Kirk didn't hesitate to break the Plexiglas protecting the studio's biggest titles.

"Get as much meat off the bone as you can."

I cracked my knuckles and got ready for a tornado. Remember, there were three major broadcasters at the time, and they had all been banging on my door for years to make this very deal. I was about to make one network very happy and its two competitors very, very angry. I called ABC, NBC, and CBS and said that I was willing to sell all three titles. When they asked me how much I wanted, I threw the pressure back on them.

"You tell me what you're willing to pay, and I'll respond to you before the end of the day."

My goal was to obtain three competing offers that I could pit against one another for maximum leverage. After weeks of painful back-and-forth, I squeezed the most amount of money out of NBC, and we inked the licensing contracts. As expected, the losers were incensed. Barry

Diller, who was in charge of negotiating broadcast rights for ABC, developed a particularly strong hatred toward me.

"I'll get you back for this," he barked when he found out that I had made the deal with NBC. Barry's tirade was just the tip of the iceberg; I succeeded in royally pissing off Lew Wasserman.

"You're Judas!" Lew screamed at me. "I trained you. . . how could you do this to the business?!"

"Let me tell you something—"

"*You're* gonna tell ME something?!"

"Remember Bill Goetz and *Winchester '73*?" I shot back. "I took this straight out of your playbook."

People won't stay angry if you have something to sell.

It isn't wise to make a habit out of pissing off your colleagues, but that doesn't mean you shouldn't go all in when the deck is stacked in your favor. With a sale as colossal as MGM's top films, I needed to milk the cow for all she was worth, despite the backlash I knew I'd receive. In the wake of my supposed betrayal, Lew took our standing lunch off the books for a few months. But once he needed a favor from me again, he acted as if the NBC deal had never occurred. In the heat of the moment, you have to expect that the people opposite you are going to flip out. Never forget that entertainment is an intimidation game, and the best salespeople don't get rattled.

Even after we sold off our most valuable titles, Kirk's casinos always weighed heavy on our studio. We were shackled in debt, and the banks fixed their eyes on our financial activity like hawks on mice. One afternoon my secretary burst into my office, insisting that the head of accounts at Chemical Bank needed to speak to me. Not good news. . . Chemical Bank handled all of Kirk's loans for resort construction. I had never masqueraded as a hospitality executive, and I had no interest in starting now. But Kirk was off the grid and Frank Rosenfelt was nowhere to be found. I was the third in command at MGM, and, according to my secretary, Chemical Bank was about to foreclose on our loan. I picked up my phone and got ready for a fresh game of Thrillseekers.

"Is this Harris Katleman?"

"Sure is."

"You have violated the covenant of the MGM loan," the man declared. "We have no choice but to foreclose."

"What the hell are you talking about?"

"We made it expressly clear that you could not reduce the assets of MGM until you paid back our loan."

"Who said we're reducing the assets of MGM?" I asked, genuinely puzzled.

"You think we'd let your $5 million check slide past us? We handle your accounts."

"I have no idea what you're talking about."

"Based on the circumstances, we've concluded that you sold part of MGM in an effort to remain financially afloat. Where else would $5 million come from?"

To reiterate, I hadn't the slightest clue what the bank was talking about. No one had told me anything about selling a portion of the company. I told the head of accounts that I would call him back and reached out to Al Benedict, the president of the MGM Grand.

"Al, did we sell a piece of MGM?" I asked.

"Of course we didn't. What's the question?"

"Chemical Bank's about to renege on our loan. Supposedly Kirk cashed a check for $5 million, and they smell a rat."

"Oh, that check? Came from Adnan Khashoggi. He had a bad night at the baccarat table, let me tell you."

If you know anything about the international weapons trade, you'll recognize Adnan Khashoggi's name. He was the world's biggest arms dealer from the 1960s through the 1980s, brokering monstrous deals between America and the Middle East. A bald, paunchy man of Turkish descent, he wore a trimmed mustache and fine suits. Khashoggi built his $14 billion empire on the principle of extravagance. In a 2009 interview with the *New York Times*, he stated about his spending habits, "It is all part of the mechanism for impressing people, with your talk, with your views, and with your appearance." At Khashoggi's peak, he spent $250,000 each day to maintain his style of living. Once, he held a party at his villa in Marbella that spanned five days and has since been considered the most extravagant event in European history. I didn't make the guest list for that one, but years prior I had the pleasure of spending an afternoon on the *Nabila*, Khashoggi's 281-foot yacht named after his daughter. In addition to being featured in the James Bond film *Never Say Never Again*, the $100 million boat has passed through the ownership of the sultan of Brunei, Donald Trump, and Prince Al-Waleed bin Talal.

Khashoggi had cruised down the coast of the French Riviera for the Cannes International Film Festival and invited Kirk aboard. He didn't object to Kirk's plus two: myself and Cary Grant. The boat was unbelievable. The top deck had more beautiful women than a party at the Playboy mansion. Khashoggi gave me, Kirk, and Cary a private tour of the vessel, through the A-plus kitchen and dining hall, the lavish rooms, and ornate lounges.

"Why don't you show Cary and Harris your stateroom?" Kirk suggested.

Along with a particularly stunning French girl, Khashoggi led us to the stern, where double steel doors stretched from the floor to the ceiling. It had a turnstile on it: a massive safe.

"Would you mind?" Khashoggi said softly, and we all turned our backs as he spun the knob.

Khashoggi swung the doors open to illuminate a wall of metal drawers, each one individually labeled. Cartier, Harry Winston, Tiffany, Van

Cleef & Arpels—the arms dealer had a bank of jewels aboard. He caressed the woman on his arm.

"Which one would you like today?"

"I don't know," she chimed.

"Close your eyes and point your finger," he said. The girl obeyed with a smile on her face, letting her pointer finger wander over the drawers. It hovered over Piaget, and she opened her eyes. Khashoggi opened the drawer and offered a diamond necklace to the girl.

Luckily, I only got to witness the fun side of Khashoggi—not the ruthless side. He has been involved in every major military scandal of the century, most notably the Iran-Contra affair, in which he sold arms to Iran in exchange for American hostages. Khashoggi worked for anyone with money, regardless of political standpoint. "My personal philosophy," he has stated publicly, "is I don't regret matters that happen, good or bad."

Knowing Adnan Khashoggi as a die-hard adrenaline junkie, Al Benedict's story made all the sense in the world. Khashoggi had lost $5 million to Kirk's casino, and when the accountants deposited the check, Chemical Bank had assumed that Kirk sold a portion of the hotel. In other words, the bank's threats were founded on hot air. I called back the head of accounts to set the record straight.

"If you foreclose on us, you better have $10 billion in assets," I told him when he answered, "because that's what we'll sue you for." He apologized sincerely after I explained the circumstance to him. "Next time, take a look at the check before calling me with idle threats. It has Adnan Khashoggi's name on it."

Over the years to follow, the Khashoggi name would encompass more than the weapons trade. Adnan's nephew, Jamal Khashoggi, became a prominent journalist for the *Washington Post* before being murdered at Istanbul's Saudi Arabian consulate in 2018. I think it's safe to say that Jamal lived a more honorable life than his uncle.

Reflecting back on the licensing deals that I made during my days at MGM, we really did liquidate the company. Kirk used the studio as a means to source his real legacy: the resort business. Hollywood gave him a lot of heat for his impact on the industry. I think his detractors lack perspective. Like all great moguls, Kirk threw out the rule book and made decisions that benefited himself and his stockholders. If that meant selling his eighty-year-old studio to a massive conglomerate, then so be it. I think his utter disregard for material possessions stemmed from his upbringing; he had gotten along just fine without life's bells and whistles. He chose a Pontiac Firebird over a private chauffeur and bought movie tickets to films he financed, maintaining that he didn't want to owe any favors. Kirk was never sentimental and never nostalgic—he had no problem selling a prized asset, whether it be the 1945 Cessna that kickstarted his career, the MGM Grand, or Dorothy's ruby slippers.

Know when to throw out the manual.

Most major industries have a clear sequence of steps to take in order to ascend. If you want to be a doctor (God help you), you have to take about a million science courses, ace the MCAT, attend medical school, and complete a residency program. The entertainment business, however, has no such track. In Hollywood, you'll find people with backgrounds in anything from politics to underwater basket weaving. This appeals to those who hate school, love the beaches, and want to make a boatload of money. But as one of those people myself, I can assure you that the aimless nature of the business makes it all the more challenging to navigate.

Following the rules isn't the recipe to breaking boundaries. Take, for instance, a quintessential goody two-shoes: a student who does exactly what his teachers tell him in high school. He participates in class, turns in his homework on time, and aces every exam. Would you bet on him becoming a Wall Street executive, a Hollywood studio head, or a high school teacher? I'd hedge a hefty bet that he'll have papers to grade in his professional future. Don't get me wrong—teaching is an honorable profession. But it won't allow you to affect the trends of modern business, and it won't back a collection of Rolexes.

If you want to be a rainmaker in any major industry, you need to master the craft of the business. . . and then you need to break it. Think about Pablo Picasso. Though he's famous for his abstract work that breaks every rule of art, he started out painting hyperrealistic works like the countless traditionalists who came before him. Once Picasso achieved mastery over his craft, he created his own signature style that revolutionized the field. The same principle applies to entertainment. Once you figure out how the business works, start breaking the rules. The industry is destined to evolve—it's up to you to be a part of that evolution.

Presiding over MGM Television offered new power, new responsibility, and new opportunity—all of which I loved. More, I earned success with shows like *CHiPs* and *How the West Was Won* and TV movies like *Babe*. MGM had grown from a laughingstock into the third most successful television outfit, behind Universal and Paramount. But when I compared my producers' compensation to my own, I couldn't help but feel snubbed. They were making nearly triple my salary, and they all came to me for advice. When I asked Frank Rosenfelt for a raise, he whined that MGM couldn't afford to boost my salary.

"Are you forgetting that I manage my division's profits?" I asked. "We made a killing last year."

But arguing with Frank was less productive than sweet-talking a cement wall. I resolved to take up the issue with Kirk, largely to the same effect. He offered a ton of company stock but refused to budge on my salary.

"Any producer can have a good year or two, but you're the president of a studio," Kirk said.

"Better I shouldn't be!" was my response.

I enjoyed the sizzle of my position, but the sleepless nights and crushing stress weren't worth my pay. As much as I revered Kirk, his infatuation with the business of Las Vegas weighed on my ability to produce outstanding material. In order to make it to the next level, I had to take another leap of faith. Not a preemptive one, as I'd taken under the trance of David Charnay. If I was going to leave MGM, it would be to work with someone I could trust. That would turn out to be the CEO of Columbia Pictures, Alan Hirschfield.

An Okie by birth, Alan drooled over Hollywood. He was slim and managerial, with a thin nose and watery eyes. Alan understood the phrase "work hard, play hard," running studios by day and slamming shots with celebrities by night. Alan wasn't a mentor like Lew Wasserman, an idea man like Mark Goodson, or a mogul like Kirk Kerkorian. He was an avid socialite with a knack for putting the right people in the same room.

I met Alan Hirschfield at a producer's dinner party in 1978. I had heard a lot about the finance genius who had saved Warner Bros. before becoming the CEO of Columbia Pictures. Looking at him in the flesh, it struck me how fully he captured the attentions of the table. It's typically easy to sniff out Los Angeles natives from transplants, but Alan had just as much Hollywood in his veins as the talent. He and I hit it off from the get-go. We shared not only the same idea of success, but a common philosophy on how to achieve it.

There's always room for another friend.

In an industry built on social connections, it often feels like there aren't enough hours in the day to forge a new friendship. With the workday filled with an endless onslaught of calls and meetings, you often find yourself dreading the idea of meeting a new person. But in Hollywood, you never know what someone might be able to do for you. Not only did Alan prove to be the friend of a lifetime, he paved the way for my transition to Columbia Pictures and Fox. Who knows what would have happened if I kept him as an acquaintance? I could have ended up working at one of Kirk's casinos in Las Vegas.

After graduating from the University of Oklahoma and Harvard Business School, Alan started his Wall Street career at an investment banking firm called Allen & Company. His social ease camouflaged his status as a financial prodigy. Alan could crunch numbers like nobody's business, and he treated spreadsheets like poetry. Oddly, when Alan wasn't staring at complex numbers or graphs, he was collecting Native American art—tapestries, arrowheads—you name it. He used to say that if he couldn't live in New York, he'd buy a cabin in the mountains of Wyoming where he could study American Indian culture. Everyone has their passions, I suppose.

Alan's superiors at the firm tasked him to open an office in Paris when he was twenty-six years old. Alan set up a thriving French business for the company, and within a year he returned to New York to delve into the Four Star Productions account. Mind you, this was years before my scuffle with David Charnay. Alan consulted for Four Star when the company was still being run by its titular four stars. As actors, they had flushed the company's finances down the tubes, and Alan devoted his energies to returning the company to a financially secure condition. As I think on it, his success led to my misstep with that company years later. If Four Star's finances didn't look so good, I wouldn't have been seduced to work for Charnay after my tenure at Goodson Todman.

The entertainment world took notice of Alan's talents after he stabilized Four Star. He went to work for a company called Seven Arts Entertainment, which aimed to acquire leasing rights to film libraries. Alan became the middleman between major motion picture companies and television networks; he specialized in deals that allowed movies to broadcast on television. It was the same business model that Kirk and I used to bail MGM out of its resort debt.

While at Seven Arts, Alan learned that Jack Warner was looking to sell Warner Bros.. The burgeoning television business had crucified Warner

Bros., along with most motion picture companies, and Jack was ready to wave his white flag. Contrarily, Alan wanted in; at the age of twenty-nine, he found himself making a play to buy one of Hollywood's major film studios.

Warner Bros. owned a number of smaller companies including two prominent record labels: Warner and Reprise. As Alan neared the goal line of finalizing Seven Arts' purchase of Warner Bros., he realized that the famed crooner Frank Sinatra owned 33.3 percent of each label. To make the books stack up correctly, Alan persuaded Frank to drop his ownership down to 20 percent, on the condition that all additional company acquisitions—and Alan emphasized that there would be many—would be at no cost to Frank. Sinatra obliged, and the deal closed. With the power of Warner Bros. behind him, Alan went on to purchase Atlantic Records, which boasted clients such as Aretha Franklin, Cream, and Led Zeppelin. A larger conglomerate called Warner Communications bought Warner Seven Arts within three years, and Frank Sinatra collected a check for $25 million: the largest clump of money he ever received in his life.

As Alan's next pet project, he took on the flailing Columbia Pictures. After observing the financial renaissance of Warner Bros. under Alan's leadership, the studio handpicked him to review its accounts. In addition to being one of the great film studios, Columbia owned a number of prolific music and commercial companies, but poor management had crippled the company. Alan believed that the company was unsalvageable and advised that the senior partners liquidate the company. But it wasn't that easy. Wedged into a business enslaved to appearance, the board refused to admit that it was on the brink of bankruptcy. So for the sake of image, Alan agreed to step in as the new CEO of Columbia Pictures. In his new post, he would quietly liquidate without alerting the attentions of Hollywood. He underestimated, however, his effectiveness in transforming the company. By reducing spending, selling assets, and exploring new avenues for film financing, Alan realized that liquidation might no longer be necessary. He had resurrected Columbia Pictures by accident.

When I first met Alan, Columbia was reflecting growth in each of its sectors save for television, which was being run by my friend Larry White. By the token of coincidence, Larry had developed content at Goodson Todman for a hot second before becoming the vice president of daytime programming at NBC.

Alan knew that he needed to resuscitate a wilting television department. In the late 1970s, the medium of television was expanding overnight. Much like the digital business in the 2010s, it opened the door to untapped revenue streams. But Larry hadn't produced results, and to be frank, Alan wasn't an expert in the television business. Alan made a few calls to the town to inquire about my reputation. Within six months of the dinner party where I met him, I got a voicemail on my home phone.

"It's Alan J. Hirschfield," the recording declared. "Ring me back on a secure line."

Much to my surprise, Alan extended the opportunity to replace Larry as president of Columbia Television.

"I'm flattered," I said. "I sure would love to switch lots."

"Then put in your notice tomorrow—I want you here as soon as possible."

"Can't do it," I replied. "Larry White's my friend."

"Larry doesn't have a show on the air. Sometimes the cow has to eat the cabbage."

But for me, loyalty was the only thing that didn't have a price tag. As sick as I was of locking horns with Frank Rosenfelt and bailing out MGM's resort debts, I couldn't sell my friend down the river. Alan didn't give up. Within a week, I came home to another voice mail on my answering machine, offering an overall production deal with Columbia. As a producer with a first-look deal at the studio, I would feed content into Larry's division and hopefully boost the studio's numbers. If Larry couldn't turn the studio around within two years, I would take his place.

"No one gets hurt with this arrangement," Alan said.

"All right, on one condition. Larry White has to be entirely aware of my presence."

"Larry's dying for you to come over!" Alan exclaimed. It made sense— Larry needed producers that could amp up the performance of the studio. He also trusted that I didn't carry a rusty dagger in my pocket.

Protect your relationships.

Despite the excitement of a new company or the intrigue of a salary hike, relationships are the most important currency in Hollywood. The people who burn bridges in their ascent through the business are typically fated to an early retirement. People in Hollywood don't forget breaches of trust, and what goes around comes around. But aside from the chance of betrayals backfiring on your career, you don't want to be the token Hollywood greaseball who doesn't understand the principle of integrity. After all, the people in your life are more important than the title of your job.

Though I kept my enthusiasm secret, I couldn't wait to start my own production company. It's difficult to explain the stresses of running a studio. You're responsible and accountable for every error throughout the genesis of a show, whether it stems from the writing, acting, or production. It's really like being a rat on the wheel—no matter how long or how hard you try, you can never achieve absolute success. Perhaps that's why it's so addicting. I've always been interested by the ways in which people deal with power. We crave it; we'll step on throats in order to obtain it. But once we acquire it—if we're lucky enough to do so—we mourn the passing of a simpler life.

As I prepared for life as a producer, I remembered how difficult it was generating concepts at Goodson Todman. A wise friend of mine once told me that intelligence is defined by self-awareness. I knew I wasn't cut out to thrive creatively. I was a good outside man with sales and packaging acumen, but if I wanted my new company to soar, I needed an inside man in the writers' room.

I milled through a number of options before deciding upon Harve Bennett as a creative partner. I had first met Harve when he was an executive at ABC. He had gone on to executive produce two legendary television series: *Rich Man, Poor Man* and *The Six Million Dollar Man*. The first title, starring Peter Strauss and Nick Nolte, followed the colorful lives of two brothers—one of whom rose from nothing to construct a corporate empire and another who became a rebellious boxer. *The Six Million Dollar Man* was the fusion of James Bond and Inspector Gadget, following a bionic man who worked as the government's secret agent. Not only had Harve realized success in the industry, he had done so with two completely different types of programming: a historical drama that spanned decades and an action fantasy. More, Harve was a reliable partner. I had seen executives clash—most prominently Mark and Bill clawing at each other like rabid squirrels—and I couldn't imagine a similar future with Harve. We shook hands and got ready to move into a set of newly minted offices on the Columbia lot. I had one last piece of business to attend to: tendering my resignation to Kirk.

"I hope you understand," I told him, sitting in his office. He flashed his bemused smile.

"Nothing is sacred."

Just like that, my days at MGM were over. As I left the lot a final time, I reflected on how grateful I was to the inimitable Kirk Kerkorian. He was my lifeline, providing the opportunity to jump from unemployed to studio president. Kirk taught me two invaluable lessons that I needed to internalize before succeeding as a studio president. First off: despite the glamour of Hollywood, cold, hard business underpins the industry. And second: always bet on the person who had a tougher upbringing. The fat cats are bound to fold when the going gets tough.

A New Company and a New Scandal
1977–1980

With a new studio, new bosses, and a new job, I was back to producing. This time, I wasn't fighting the leash of Goodson Todman's game show brand. Nor was I working for a studio looking to do business on the cheap, as I'd experienced under Kirk's regime at MGM. As an Emmy-winning writer and the former president of MGM Television, Harve and I were the white knights at Columbia, and Alan Hirschfield made sure that our treatment reflected that status. The studio spent thousands on the offices of Bennett Katleman Productions, giving us half a floor in the television building on the Columbia/Warner Bros. lot in Burbank. We had secretaries, private bathrooms, kitchens—you name it. Hollywood had never tasted any sweeter. In those years, Alan and I were scoundrels together— two executives savoring the pleasures of Hollywood. I remember him calling me with a trickle of shame in his voice one afternoon.

"Spit it out," I said.

"Do you remember a girl by the name of Blake?" he asked. Blake was a drop-dead gorgeous model whom I had dated a few years prior.

"Of course I do."

"What would you tell me—hypothetically, of course—if I told you I was seeing her?"

"Go with God," I said.

Alan was madly in love with his wife, Berte, but when it came to women, he couldn't help himself. He was like a kid in a candy shop with all of the starlets and sirens of Hollywood. Berte had heard whisperings of his adultery, but she overlooked his peccadilloes time and time again.

A few weeks into Alan and Blake's fling, Alan's father flew into Los Angeles to stay with the Hirschfields for a week. Of course, he wasn't privy to Alan's philandering, and Alan wasn't going to stop seeing his girl of the month just because his father was sleeping in his guest bedroom. My number must have been lying around the Hirschfields' house, because Alan's father called around 2:00 a.m.

"Where the hell is Alan?!"

"I haven't a clue—probably the office," I replied.

"I know your game," said Alan's father. "If he's not home in thirty minutes, I'm calling the cops."

My suspicions were confirmed when I dialed Blake; Alan was shacked out at her condo in West Hollywood.

"Blake, can I speak with Alan?"

"He's indisposed at the moment," she said, stoned out of her mind.

"Do me a favor and tell him his daddy wants him to come home," I told her.

At the office, I had one political problem to deal with. Remember David Begelman, the New York–based MCA agent that I fired for embezzling money under Lew Wasserman's nose? He had managed to fail upward, and now he was running Columbia's motion picture department. In fact, his run of smash hits had kept Columbia afloat since Alan Hirschfield's takeover of the company. Having green-lit titles like *Close Encounters of the Third Kind*, *Taxi Driver*, and *Kramer vs. Kramer*, David was operating at a peak level.

Considering that David's last words to me had been "I'll get you back, mother fucker," I figured he probably harbored some resentment toward me. I'd feel the same way if a twenty-three-year-old kid ended my eleven-year streak at MCA. To my bewilderment, David let bygones be bygones and supported my move to Columbia.

I learned the value of charm working with David—he was as smooth as they come. With creased eyes and a large rudder of a nose, he was the

Me and my three children: Steven Katleman, Lisa Sherman, Me, and Michael Katleman

Ron Meyer, Ellen Meyer, Michael Ovitz, and Judy Ovitz

Glen A. Larson and Alan Hirschfield

The Davis family: John Davis, Marvin Davis, and Barbara Davis

Me with Rupert Murdoch

Sherry Lansing and Me

With the cast of of **LA Law** *(left to right)*
Top row: *Alan Rachins, Steven Bochco, Jill Eikenberry, Michael Tucker, Susan Dey, Greg Hoblit, Unknown, Larry Drake, Jonathan Dolgen* **Bottom row:** *Richard Dysart, Corbin Bernsen, Me, Blair Underwood*

Susan Wright, Bob Wright, Me, Lilly Tartikoff, and Brandon Tartikoff

Greg Hoblit, Steven Bochco, Me, and Rupert Murdoch

Me with Beldon Katleman

Me with Grace Kelly, Marty Pasetta

Me with President Gerald Ford

With the stars of **Anything But Love**: *Jamie Lee Curtis, Me, and Richard Lewis*

Kirk Kerkorian

Mark Goodson

Lew Wasserman

Bill Todman

Dennis Stanfill

Bill Haber

Bob Iger

type of guy who made you want him to like you. He also understood the value of appearance in the nucleus of superficiality. Knowing that stars wanted to work with distinguished bookworms, David fabricated that he had a degree from Yale. As far as I know, he barely squeaked through high school. But David's little tricks always worked. No matter how much money you had, he wouldn't let you pick up the check at dinner. He gave every waiter his credit card before dining; that way, the restaurant could charge him with a 20 percent tip at the end of meals without any fuss. His guests used to call it the Begelman Touch. If he knew it was your birthday and you liked pistachios, he wouldn't mail you a bag; he'd have a hundred pounds of green nuts delivered to your doorstop. Years later when I tried to sign Johnny Carson to Fox, I took a play straight out of David's book by having my secretary order one hundred boxes of fortune cookies for Johnny that read, "You will sign with Twentieth Century Fox," on prophetic slips of paper. I failed to harness the Begelman Touch because Johnny signed with Columbia, but that's a different story.

Despite his success, David hadn't abandoned the seedy practices I witnessed in MCA's New York office. He had a serious gambling problem and was up to his eyeballs in debt. Every week, he flocked to a private room at Mr. Chow's restaurant, where he joined Hollywood's high-stakes poker games. I'd like to say I have icy veins, but that game was way too much for me. Executives would bet upward of $50,000 in a single hand, and the game ran all night. David was among the chumps, losing far more hands than he ever won.

Kirk Kerkorian secretly lent well over $100,000 to David, but it was never enough. For every dollar made, he spent fifty. Though David was a snake-oil salesman by nature, he became a real crook when desperation set in. He betrayed his clients and friends to keep creditors at bay, but he could never yank the debt monkey off his back. In fact, he allegedly pocketed massive chunks of Judy Garland's checks while representing her at the boutique agency he started after leaving MCA. After Judy had been hospitalized for a drug overdose, he regretfully told her that the paparazzi had snapped a photograph of her stomach being pumped. Judy cared about her public image and implored David for advice on destroying the image.

"The photographer's demanding a ransom," David said regretfully. "I'm afraid it's the only way."

Of course the story was fake; David immediately drained the money at a Vegas craps table. How on Earth did David operate at a high level with so many secrets? Who's to say—how did JFK hide his romance with Marilyn Monroe? How did Arnold Schwarzenegger serve two terms as the governor of California without revealing that he knocked up his nanny? Everyone has ghosts—some people are just better at hiding them.

I had heard rumblings of David's money problems, but I had no interest digging up gossip. Columbia had spent thousands to make me comfortable, and now it was time to scratch the studio's back with big numbers. While everyone aspires to be a Hollywood producer, no one ever discusses the difficulties behind getting a project off the ground. Whereas writers work their way out of unemployment, directors execute a creative vision, and studio executives handle the financials, producers are professional puzzle solvers, piecing together the right people and components. But they don't spearhead creative efforts, and they don't control the cash flow. To that effect, it can take a minute for a producer to get the wheels rolling. Especially when launching a new production outfit, you need allies at the studio to shepherd projects through the production process. To my misfortune, my allies were gone within a month of my arrival on the lot.

In 1978, the Academy Award–winning actor Cliff Robertson received a 1099 form from Columbia Pictures indicating $10,000 in earnings. Cliff had never seen the money. He reached out to the studio and sparked an investigation that unveiled $65,000 in checks forged by David Begelman himself. As the CEO of Columbia Pictures, Alan Hirschfield resolved to fire Begelman on moral grounds, but the crooked executive wasn't willing to go down quietly. David Begelman was fast friends with Herbert Allen, the CEO of Allen & Company, who maintained a controlling stake in the studio. Herbert offered David an extended vacation to "clear his mind." He figured that the political crisis would blow over by the time David returned, but he underestimated the obstinacy of Alan Hirschfield. Alan had lost all trust in Begelman and demanded immediate termination. In the end, it came down to a rock, paper, scissors game of firing. Hirschfield canned Begelman, and Begelman convinced Herbert Allen to fire Hirschfield. I had to watch from the sidelines as everyone bit the dust.

You can imagine the vitriol between Alan and David. But as occurs often in Hollywood, both of them failed upward. Alan would land at Fox, where he supplanted the reigning CEO. David Begelman, much to the shock of the town, became the CEO of MGM. I suppose Kirk had developed a soft spot for him after all those years of shelling out money. But Begelman had lost his mojo—he wasn't able to drum up any profits and was quietly fired before his contract expired. In August of 1995, David checked into the Century Plaza Hotel under the name Bruce Vann. He invited his mistress Sandra Bennett, Tony Bennett's ex-wife, to his suite, where they had an exchange that left Sandra questioning his state of mind. After Sandra headed home, David messengered a number of letters to his remaining friends and shot himself in the head with a .38-caliber pistol. For the first time in decades, he was debt-free.

Appearances can be deceiving.

Was David Begelman a good man? Of course not. But I have to hand it to him: he managed to hide a history of reprehensible behavior beneath a seamless veneer of grace. As I reflect, it occurs to me that a sense of calm amid chaos—an ability to keep multiple plates spinning at once—is the key to surviving the tumult of Hollywood. David was destined to fail, but he staved off the inevitable for much longer than most people could have managed.

It should also be noted that David wasn't—and isn't—the only person in Hollywood capable of hiding skeletons. Even if someone looks the part, keep an eye out. You never *really* know a person, especially in show business.

Eighteen years before David's tragic end, I found myself alone at Columbia, without the two men who had advocated for my presence on the lot. I could feel the flames licking at me, and I didn't have the first clue what our first show would be. We weren't given guidelines on demographic or subject matter; Columbia just needed wide profit margins. Though generating material fell within Harve Bennett's creative responsibilities, it became imminently clear that he wasn't necessary a wellspring of original ideas. Both *Rich Man, Poor Man* and *The Six Million Dollar Man* had been adaptations based on best-selling novels. And so I found myself experiencing déjà vu. Just as when I started at MGM, I had to figure out which stories I would tell to mainstream America. I reverted to what had worked at MGM. . .

When in doubt, raid the library.

My desperation for a signature project sent me flipping through Columbia's filmography in search of a classic film to adapt. Lo and behold, my eyes snagged upon a familiar title: *From Here to Eternity*. The Oscars-sweeping film that I had sold over twenty years ago was a Columbia picture. The movie had launched my career at MCA; why not stick with what works?

Original ideas with commercial potential are often in short supply. Luckily, Hollywood has a deep archive of stories that are available for the milking. The trick to cracking a good adaptation is twofold: first, make sure that enough time has elapsed between the original and the remake, and second, be certain that the new take adds flair to the source material. Sometimes you're better off returning to what works than trying to reinvent the wheel.

As Harve and I began working on our television adaptation, we stumbled upon a serious issue with respect to story structure. While *From Here to Eternity* had a firm beginning, middle, and end, the television version needed to be open-ended, as we had no clue how many seasons the show would ultimately last. The challenge effectively stumped our writers, who failed to see how the title could sustain a television series. So Harve and I decided to make a miniseries instead of a full series. From there, we would see how the public responded.

With Columbia holding the rights and Harve working on the scripts, I focused on the casting process. Television adaptations always need an exemplary cast; if you have two-bit playhouse actors reprising classic roles, the production looks like a joke. To replace the original film's cast, I secured deals with major stars including Bill Devane, Natalie Wood, Kim Basinger, Joe Pantoliano, and Peter Boyle. The miniseries was an instant hit—so much so that NBC immediately ordered a full series. With our first show on the air, Bennett Katleman Productions had proved its salt to the powers of Columbia. We were still nervous about how we were going to skew the title into an open-ended format, but with NBC dangling money in our faces, we had to pull through.

"Write now, worry later," I told Harve.

I had already pieced together a dynamite cast; now I just had to hold on to them. Little did I know that I'd nearly come to blows with Bill Devane's agent Jonathan Gaines. With the exception of Natalie Wood (whom I replaced with the *Partridge Family* star Susan Dey), most of the actors wanted to return for the series. But Gaines smelled the scent of money in the breeze. Once the entire cast agreed to a fixed raise for the full series, Gaines demanded an extra $100,000 per episode for Bill. Needless to say, I blew a gasket. Gaines had purposefully waited for all the other deals to close; that way, we'd have no choice but to roll over and give him the extra cash. As a former agent, I knew Gaines's thought process, and I wasn't going to let him push me around.

"You have no sense of morality," I told him over the phone. "I'll replace Devane before the week's through."

Of course I was bluffing—Bill Devane was the figurehead of the show, and we needed him. As much as I hate to admit it, Gaines had all the leverage. The next week, we had a high-octane meeting in my office. Instead of a lounge area, I had a twelve-person table planted in the middle of my office, and I remember shooting daggers at Gaines from across its length. When he refused to compromise on his client's fee, I lost my temper and leaped across the table. Barry Lowen, my voice of reason, had to restrain me.

"I'll dance on your grave," I said after agreeing to Bill's extra $75,000 per episode.

If you want fair, go to Pomona.

Anyone who stays in entertainment long enough will learn that it isn't a fair business, at least in the traditional sense. My thought is that you get what you sign up for. Hollywood doesn't follow an objective code of ethics—that's what makes it the Wild West of industries.

My blood still boils when I think back on Jonathan Gaines hijacking the production of *From Here to Eternity*. But the truth is that he did what any good agent would do: he got a max deal for his client. It would have made my life a hell of a lot easier if Gaines would have accepted a small pay bump for Bill Devane, but he had no allegiance to me. He was carrying out a fiduciary obligation to his client and himself, and I happened to be on the losing end of the fight.

If you're interested in a career on the transactional side of the entertainment business, take a close look at what the job entails. Screwing people over is a primary part of the job description, and you need to be willing to make enemies for the sake of your business. But if you're willing to do what it takes—short of becoming a supervillain, of course—you're bound for the most colorful vocation in the corporate world.

To my dismay, *From Here to Eternity* got canceled after its first season. I still blame NBC for its failure. The network swapped its airtime around several times, which precluded the show from cultivating a loyal fan base.

"If you want failure, go to NBC," I told Larry White once we heard that the show was finished. "The Vietnam War lasted longer than anything they put on." My only consolation was that Jonathan Gaines would no longer accumulate commissions.

In addition to *From Here to Eternity*, Harve and I got two other series on the air. The first was *Salvage 1*; it followed Harry Broderick, a scrapyard owner who piloted a number of moon expeditions in search of valuable space junk. The program slotted into a new genre: grounded, elevated science fiction. We got Andy Griffith to star as the protagonist, and the show resonated with critics and audiences alike. Our next program appealed to a demographic with lower tastes. Let's face it—*The American Girls* was a tits and ass show. It tracked two drop-dead beautiful journalists palling around town. Think *60 Minutes* with a Playboy spin. James Aubrey would have been proud; we had brought his "broads, bosoms, and fun" formula to television screens.

Keep a Chevy line for the masses and a Cadillac line for the snobs.

The best television executives have a sixth sense of what the public wants to watch. If you think about it, it's next to impossible to find a single show that threads the needle for all American audiences. If you can drum up a television concept that appeals to an NRA advocate from

Texas and a gender studies professor from New York City, then you should get your ass to Hollywood.

Rather than wasting my time searching for a unicorn television concept, I focused on developing content for niche demographics. That way, Harve and I were able to cover the full gamut of American tastes. *American Girls* ultimately became our Chevy line, while *From Here to Eternity* and *Salvage 1* were our Cadillacs. With a diverse slate of programming, our shows connected with viewers from every corner of the country—and the ratings reflected it.

The short stint of success I experienced at Bennett Katleman Productions was a bright spot in my career. With 50 percent ownership of every show we produced, my former salary gripes were put to rest. And as a television producer, I could make it home by six o'clock every night if we weren't shooting—a perk that positively impacted my dating life. I hate to indulge the stereotype of a Hollywood sleaze, but my story wouldn't be complete if I didn't factor in at least a few snippets of my love life. Having been married five times, I've faced my share of rough-and-tumble relationships. After my divorce from Carole, I had a fling with the famed actress Kim Basinger after I cast her in *From Here to Eternity*. She asked me out, believe it or not, which inspired me to abandon my cardinal rule of avoiding actresses cast in my shows. Kim rolled into my driveway in a white Corvette that the producer Aaron Spelling had gifted her. When I answered the door, she was holding two pairs of Rollerblades.

"Let's leave the Corvette and skate to dinner."

Let me clarify that my house is perched on a steep hill above Beverly Hills. It's not exactly Mount Crumpit, but it's not something you want to barrel down without brakes. But what was I supposed to do, say no to Kim Basinger? We nearly broke our necks rolling down that hill. Even worse was the hike back up after we'd gorged on food and wine.

My relationships didn't always end the way I'd planned. I remember a particularly sticky situation with my good friend Ronald Waranch, a real estate tycoon who developed one of the largest shopping centers in Honolulu. Ronald's claim to wealth was a series of trailer parks located on the outskirts of Los Angeles—or at least what *used* to be the outskirts of Los Angeles. When the city expanded at an exponential rate, Ronald's developments were worth tens of millions. The two of us were nearly as obsessed with golf as we were with our jobs, which sent us down to the La Costa Golf Tournament in Carlsbad, California. Ronald took the liberty of driving, as he had a beautiful Rolls-Royce among his fleet of luxury cars. When the engine started making odd noises, Ronald pulled into the Rolls-Royce dealer in Newport Beach.

"We have to order a new part," the dealer told us. "We can set you up with a rental in the meantime."

"How about I trade in this hunk of metal for that one?" Ronald asked, pointing toward a gorgeous new Corniche with marble floors.

"That model costs $250,000." Ronald whipped out his checkbook, and the two of us went rolling out of the lot on new wheels.

My weekend of excess didn't end there. After the tournament, I found myself tangled up in the sheets with a woman whom I met in the hotel bar that evening. The next morning, I got a call from none other than Beldon Katleman.

"Cuz—are you at La Costa?" he asked.

"Yeah."

"Did you fuck a girl named Bonnie?"

"Yep."

"Get the fuck out of there—that's Moe Dalitz's girlfriend!"

If you aren't familiar, Moe Dalitz was one of the most notorious bootleggers in American history. A close contemporary of mobsters like Al Capone, Lucky Luciano, and Meyer Lansky, Moe was tied up with the notorious Purple Gang based out of Detroit. Aside from Moe's unsavory affiliations, I knew that when Beldon told you to run, you listen.

I promptly packed my bags and hopped into a cab from Carlsbad to Beverly Hills.

My next dating escapade involved the actress Barbara Bach, who was the Bond girl in Roger Moore's *The Spy Who Loved Me*. I called her up when I needed a female lead in a TV movie called *The Mask of Alexander Cross*, and somehow I convinced her to star. Barbara was the type of girl who liked to feel like a princess, and I pulled out all the stops. But shortly after I brought her to the Academy Awards, she cut things off.

"Who's the guy?" I asked.

"Don't ask questions that you don't want answered."

"I want to know."

"Ringo Starr," she said. That actually softened the blow. I can accept losing to the drummer of the Beatles.

Harve Bennett, on the other hand, didn't share my interest in dating. One morning when I walked into his office, I found his head planted in his hands. He was choking on sobs, and his cheeks were slick with tears.

I paused for an instant, wishing I hadn't interrupted Harve, but I couldn't retreat to the hallway after witnessing the broken man in front of me.

"What's the matter, Harve?" I asked, taking a seat at his desk.

"I'll never be the same," he cried. "I'm ruined."

"No one's ever ruined."

"Jane ran off with her horse trainer." Jane was Harve's wife, with whom he'd adopted two children. "I knew I shouldn't have paid for those fucking riding lessons."

Whether I'm an expert or a failure in winning back an ambivalent woman, I've had my fair share of experience. I leaned forward in my chair and slapped Harve's desk.

"We'll get her back," I said. "Who's the guy?"

"It's not a man. . . it's a woman," Harve uttered.

"You're toast."

Never hire a horse trainer.

There's a fine line between fighting tough odds and folding when your cards are bad. I parse it as follows: if you can squint out a tiny chance of success—all you need is a sliver—you have to fight. But if you know you're bound to fail, abandon ship and move on. Poor Harve didn't have a shot against an equestrian with two X chromosomes.

✺

Harve waded slowly into the dating pool, but he was never the same. His ideas dried up and his creative spark dulled. Within a few months, I grew worried about our partnership. Our business model relied on him generating fresh ideas that I could sell, and our development slate was looking rather sparse. To some extent, the demise of my production company was accredited to Jane Bennett's goddamned horse trainer. If there's a moral to this part of my life, perhaps it's this: avoid equestrian sports.

Meanwhile, I'd kept up my friendship with Alan Hirschfield after the David Begelman debacle. Steve Ross, the CEO of Warner Communications, had hired Alan as a consultant in "the Office of the President," whatever that meant. Ross had assembled high-ranking money men to help with important transactional decisions, and Alan was enjoying the benefits of wielding the CEO's power without any of the accountability.

"I'd make you president of Warner Bros. Television," he told me over lunch once. "But the standing guy's doing too well."

It was only a matter of time until one of the studios poached Alan out of Steve Ross's office. Hollywood knew that Alan had a green thumb— except instead of making gardens, it made cash. In 1979, a year after Alan's dismissal from Columbia, Fox hired him as vice chairman and chief operating officer. He would serve beneath the litigious, hard-boiled CEO, Dennis Stanfill. And with only *M*A*S*H* and *Trapper John, M.D.* on the air from Fox's television department, Alan asked if I would run the division. I was game to make the jump, considering Harve Bennett was wandering our office in a lovelorn coma. In truth, the lifestyle of a producer had its perks, but I had missed the power and the perks of running a studio.

Harve stayed at Columbia for the length of our contract, but he never got another show on the air. That isn't to say that he didn't repeat the successes he had with *Six Million Dollar Man* and *Rich Man, Poor Man*; Harve wrote and produced several films in the 1980s *Star Trek* franchise. As for his love life, he rebounded with Carol, the waspiest Jewish princess I had ever met. Horse-riding lessons wouldn't be Harve's undoing this time around, but house maintenance would be. It wasn't long before Carol ran off with Harve's pool boy. I suppose that writers are destined for heartbreak.

My fourteen-year tenure at Fox spanned the privatization of the studio under oilman Marvin Davis, my battle with Dennis Stanfill, who wanted to stick my head on a spike, and the ascent of Fox Broadcasting under the leadership of Barry Diller and Rupert Murdoch. I was responsible for developing hit television shows including *The Simpsons*, *L.A. Law*, *NYPD Blue*, *Anything but Love*, *Picket Fences*, *Mr. Belvedere*, *The Tracy Ullman Show*, and *The Fall Guy*.

Alan Hirschfield assembled a crew of swashbuckling gurus as the new faces of Fox. Under Alan, Sherry Lansing handled films, I headed television, and the merchandising genius Norman Levy was in charge of distribution. We all knew the business along with the crazy, creative side of the industry. Though our take-no-prisoners attitude made the studio successful, it didn't jive with Dennis Stanfill, our chairman and CEO. Stanfill was brought in by the bankers, and he treated entertainment like a numbers business. A graduate of the Annapolis Naval Academy, Stanfill lived in San Marino and never ventured into Beverly

Hills after dark. Stanfill hated everything about us: our personalities, our attitudes, even the money we made.

I first met Dennis over dinner at a fancy restaurant in Beverly Hills. With a three-piece suit and a smug shape to his smile, he was the archetype of composure and conservativeness. I would have bet he threw out his comb, as each individual hair on his head had been trained where to fall. Dennis Stanfill was the type of man who tried running the entertainment business off a hard set of rules. Rules are great if you're selling automobiles, but they don't work when you're trying to sell television shows. If you want a program to feel fresh and unexpected, you have to be willing to throw out the manual.

Regardless, our first encounter didn't reveal our differences, and Stanfill seemed to like me just fine. I minted him as the type of boss I could skirt around. But hindsight is always twenty-twenty; I should have smelled a rat when Stanfill refused a clean break between the regime of my predecessor and that of my own. You see, Stanfill was fast friends with Russ Barry, the president whom I would replace.

"For the sake of continuity, Russ Barry will remain studio president," Dennis said. "You'll be chairman of the board." As far as I was concerned, you could have put executive custodian on my door placard as long as I called the shots.

Waltzing into Fox was much different than pulling into MGM for the first time. Fox was a much more successful company that offered more power across the board. But the television department wasn't anything short of a dumpster fire. Russ Barry was simply drawing his salary and holding an office. He cared about one thing and one thing only as he put together shows: casting. If he couldn't get A-listers, he wouldn't green-light a production. That led to very little activity, as stars typically scuttle toward the silver screen and only revert to television when they're in a slump.

TV doesn't need stars—it makes stars.

The format of a given program should determine how talent is utilized. In movies, people pay to see stars on the big screen. That means you need to cast big names like Dwayne "The Rock" Johnson if you want to succeed. But when Jane Public tunes into her favorite television show, she invites the cast and writers into her home. The public socializes with television characters on a lazy Sunday or after a long day of work. That means that story is far more important than star power. I didn't care about signing actors to my studio as Russ Barry had. Instead, I dedicated my energies to signing talented writers and producers who could execute quality stories at a high level.

This dynamic informed the way that I monitored the casting process. As a television executive, I wasn't concerned with getting big-budget actors onto my programs. In fact, I didn't think they were worth the money. I'd much rather hire a first-rate writer or director onto my show than a global superstar. A similar logic should be applied to burgeoning forms of entertainment. Take a look at the digital sphere, rugged frontier as it is. Given that our computer screens and smartphones are even more accessible than television sets, we get all but flashless stars on YouTube, Instagram, and other platforms. The premium shifts from the grandiosity to relatability.

My differences with Russ Barry extended well past casting strategy. To be frank, I couldn't stand the executives on his payroll. I'd never seen anything like it in entertainment; they would laze into the office at 9:00 a.m. and block out their calendars with 5:00 p.m. dinner reservations each night. It seemed that no one was willing to dive into the trenches and get to work. So I was presented with a choice: I could keep Russ's stable of lethargic employees, or I could clean house. One by one, I called Russ Barry's stale executives into my office and told them that I wouldn't be renewing their contracts. Per my instructions from Dennis Stanfill, I assured Russ that we could find a role for him at the company, but his ego wouldn't withstand the demotion. Within a few months, Russ and his team had vacated the lot, and I had the chance to bring in my cast of executives: Peter Grad, Ed Gradinger, Dayna Kalins, Andrea Baynes, Robert Morin, Barry Lowen, and Les Moonves.

Surround yourself with the brightest people, and you'll look like a genius.

There are two ways to go about building a team. The first involves solidifying your own power by assembling a group of lowly footmen. When you make sure that you're the brightest star in the room, you stifle potential mutinies from brewing, which should be a serious concern for the leaders of volatile industries. But I opted for a second strategy, which involved assembling the best and brightest team that I could find. I always felt that if I could beat a member of my staff in an IQ test, I had made the wrong hire. While this strategy presented an element of vulnerability to me, it allowed the studio to exceed our projections every year. Just as importantly, it allowed our office to function like an oligarchy as opposed to an autocracy, as my staff members were empowered to voice their perspectives. I received great satisfaction from promoting a healthy working environment, but I'd be remiss not to mention that my management style benefited me personally. As the leader of an all-star cast of executives, I got nods for everyone's achievements. Of course I gave credit where credit was due, but our collective success looked good to my superiors. In the end, my team's brilliance allowed me to run the studio for fourteen years, a tenure that was unprecedented in the television business. All to say: don't be afraid of sharp minds. The business is too difficult to tackle on your own, and there will be more than a handful of times when you need a room full of Einsteins to work your way out of a jam.

In addition to scouting the brightest people out there, it was a priority for me to assemble a balanced team of men and women alike. In my day, Hollywood was way too much of a sausage factory with white men dominating every corner of the business. While female executives were few and far between, I achieved great professional benefit by hiring people for their skill set as opposed to their gender. With Andrea Baynes heading development, Dayna Kalins (later Dayna Bochco) running business affairs, and Lea Stalmaster controlling the casting department, I can personally attest to the value of empowering ambitious women who want to make their mark on the industry.

Beneath Fox's massive banner, the studio only had two shows on the air when I started: *Trapper John, M.D.* and *M*A*S*H*. I had the wherewithal to understand that I played no role in the success of *M*A*S*H*, even though its profits alone were keeping my studio's lights on. During my first week on the job, I visited the set. I made it very clear to the talent and the crew that I wouldn't be disrupting their flow.

"You're pros," I told Alan Alda, who starred in the show. "Keep doing what you're doing, and let me know if there's anything you need."

"Well, there is something that's been pissing everyone off. But I don't think there's anything you could do about it."

"Try me," I said.

"It's a five-minute walk to the closest bathroom. Everyone's been dying for a bathroom onstage."

"Give me a week," I replied.

I called Mark Evans, the physical production head who had been through five different studio presidents.

"Not gonna happen, mate. Stanfill would never allow it."

As chairman of the board, I controlled a discretionary fund of $5 million. I decided to put it to good use with a state-of-the-art plumbing system exclusively for *M*A*S*H*. Days later, I got a call from Dennis Stanfill.

"I know what you're doing," he said. "Your actions will set a dangerous precedent for other shows."

"*M*A*S*H* generates millions," I responded.

"Change your course. It's against the rules."

"All right, Dennis, how about this for a rule? Any series that stays on the air for five years gets a bathroom."

Somehow, that worked. Within the week, *Entertainment Tonight* was providing coverage for the grand opening of *M*A*S*H*'s very own bathroom, and I got to cut the ribbon. I should have known that Dennis Stanfill would be seething from his home in San Marino.

About a year into the job, Alan Hirschfield called me, Sherry Lansing, and Norman Levy into his office. He was all business, shedding his devilish grin for a poker face.

"You all know that Fox is in play," he said. "We're sitting ducks—anyone can buy us."

That was all common knowledge. At the time, Fox shares were going for thirty-five dollars apiece, which was about 25 percent undervalued. The low price had attracted a number of moguls to start sniffing at the company.

"What if we took it private ourselves?"

As it turned out, Alan wasn't shooting an undeveloped idea into the wind. He and Dennis Stanfill had already secured the investment firm Wertheimer & Company as a willing underwriter. Sherry, Norman, and I were on board immediately; it would take $400 million to buy the company, but we knew that it was worth over $1 billion. This was our chance to be autonomous and have a say in our futures.

Alan Hirschfield brought his scheme to the Fox board, which immediately sparked to the idea. But the transaction opened up the question of leadership. Who would run the studio: Dennis Stanfill or Alan Hirschfield? Wertheimer & Company scheduled a meeting to discuss the future of Fox while I browsed the real estate market for homes in

Malibu. By the look on Alan's face when he returned to the office after the meeting, I knew I had gotten ahead of myself.

I wasn't in the room to recount what happened, but according to the testimonies of Alan, Wertheimer & Company supported Alan as the new CEO. While they felt that Dennis' financial acumen was beyond reproach with the purchase of Aspen, the Hoyts movie theaters, and the Coca Cola bottling company, they wanted a creative like Alan running the company. They offered Dennis the title of Chairman of the Board, but he knew that his power would be marginalized. The terms were unacceptable to Stanfill, and the deal was off.

Alan and I weren't the only people who fought to take Fox private. Our COO Joseph LaBonte might have started out as an ally of Dennis, but he became furious after failing to convince Dennis to accept the deal. The debacle eventually prompted his decision to leave Fox to become the CEO of Reebok. Even LaBonte couldn't convince Dennis to accept the deal.

Upon reflection, I believe that Dennis completely overreacted to the idea of taking Fox private. If he would have accepted his new position and allowed us to function, there would have been no Rupert Murdoch, no Fox News, and probably no President Donald J. Trump. In the end, Fox probably would have been taken over by another company, and Dennis, Alan, Norman, Sherry, and myself would have received buyouts in the tens of millions. Was Dennis a bit too zealous? I think so. But of course, that's just one man's opinion.

As I'd come to realize, Alan's failed campaign to seize power would embroil me in a major scandal. Stanfill knew that he was on shaky ground with the board publicly backing Hirschfield over himself. Hirschfield had too much power to attack directly, but his cronies were fair game. Attacking Sherry Lansing would be akin to attacking Snow White, and Norman Levy's mathematical brain protected him. That left me: the perfect target for Stanfill. It didn't help my cause that my former boss Frank Rosenfelt had publicly declared his bitter distaste for me. The second I heard about that one, I called him up to remind him that the vast majority of MGM's profits came from my television division. I may have tossed an expletive or two in there as well.

Dennis Stanfill figured that removing me would destabilize Hirschfield's ascent within the company. Ever since building the *M*A*S*H* bathroom, I could sense that he disliked me, but I didn't think much of it. I had been confident that my department's performance would secure my job. The next few months would disprove that notion.

In the autumn of 1980, I found myself in Monaco on business for *The Monte Carlo Show*, a weekly variety program that starred Patrick Wayne. During some downtime, I bought a few dresses for my then girlfriend, Katia Christine. But I made a small error when I returned stateside—I included the receipts for the clothes within my stack of restaurant bills and car service tabs. My assistant Barbara submitted my monthly expenses to our accounting department for reimbursement, and the dress charges were flagged as suspicious. Of course I immediately paid for the charges out of my own pocket once the mistake came to my attention, but it was too late. Stanfill had been licking his chops for months, and this was his moment to pounce. Within the month, I received a notice from Chuck Weiss, Stanfill's enforcer at the studio. I remember the wave of anger passing over me as I read the page. Morality clause violations, embezzlement charges, allegations of supplying Alan Hirschfield with prostitutes and drugs. It became very clear: Stanfill was out for my blood.

For the record, the charges of fraud derived from a simple accounting error. I called Alan immediately, my voice somewhere between rage and panic.

"What's going on?!" I asked.

"Let's get a coffee."

"Meet at the commissary?"

"Let's go off the lot today," Alan replied coolly. He was convinced that Dennis had tapped the phones.

"They're saying you're my drug dealer and my pimp," Alan said. "You barely drink—let alone smoke—and I don't need your help getting women."

"You better get me through this storm."

"I'll take care of it."

But Alan couldn't do much to curb Stanfill's vendetta. After all, Stanfill's real target in the whole disaster was Alan himself, whom he deemed the real threat. It was an elaborate game of who's more powerful: The king or the pope? That week, I had my assistant Barbara write an interoffice memo that explained the situation and extended a profuse apology. Dennis responded with a demand for my resignation. He gave me the "courtesy" to step down voluntarily and protect my reputation.

I had worked in Hollywood long enough to understand that the studio shuffle is all about intimidation tactics. Dennis put on a mean show, but he didn't have a single cause to fire me. All of his charges were wrongful speculation. With that in mind, I made it expressly clear that I would not be stepping down. I figured I could tolerate more pain than my tyrannical boss. Thus began a war between myself and Dennis Stanfill that would span the next eight months. Dennis had the memory of an elephant and the fight of a pit bull, and he tried everything to smoke me out of Fox. He started by pulling John Van de Kamp, the Los Angeles district attorney, into the investigation against me. I'll never forget when my lawyer, Skip Brittenham, told me that I had to present my case in front of the district attorney.

"I hate to say it," he mumbled, "but there's a chance you'll go to the slammer for this."

Mind you, this was over a $700 receipt that I covered personally. I'd be a liar to deny a brief episode of absolute panic. But then I remembered a line from the ever-wise golfing legend Arnold Palmer. I'd been lucky enough to partner with Arnold in a professional-amateur tournament in Pebble Beach, and on my first drive, I sent the ball into the thickest stock of trees on the course.

"I'm in big trouble, Arnie," I uttered.

"Big trouble is when you can't breathe. Chip it out."

Nothing like a PGA champion to provide some perspective.

Trouble is cause for action, not for panic.

Everyone goes through their fair share of catastrophes. What separates the sharks from the minnows is the capacity to remain calm and work your way out of the situation. That's easier said than done when your entire career is on the brink of going up in flames, but it's absolutely essential. From Lew Wasserman to Kirk Kerkorian to Rupert Murdoch, the smartest businesspeople I've encountered run the gamut of personalities and working styles. But they all confronted disaster in the same three-step process:

- Compose yourself.
- Handle the short-term issue rationally.
- Beat the shit out of whoever caused the problem in the first place.

Though simple on paper, this sequence is against every human instincts. In the animal kingdom, it's all about fight or flight—not calm hyperactivity. That's why great problem solvers are so rare in the workplace. It's hard not to freak out.

Anyways, I resolved to take the necessary steps to stick it out at Fox and protect myself. That started with expanding my legal counsel to include Edward Bennett Williams, who owned a piece of the Redskins and the Orioles. He had also represented Nixon throughout the Watergate scandal, so I figured his experience was adequate. The months leading up to my meeting with the DA were complete agony. Dennis whispered into the ear of the press at every turn, and I found a new media outlet defaming my reputation every week. At one point, Bill Haber commented that I had been in every publication save for *Popular Mechanics*.

Things got a bit too personal when Dennis's henchman, Chuck Weiss, called up my mother.

"Your son is a thief," he told her over the phone, which prompted her to call me in tears. You can speak to the DA, you can speak to the press, but you can't speak to my mother. I was so angry that my teeth were rattling in my skull as I dialed Chuck Weiss.

"You better keep a gun in your drawer, because I'm going to come into your office and kick the shit out of you," I told him. That was the last that my mother ever heard from Chuck or his people.

My personal hell hadn't prevented Fox from being courted by other buyers. At a board meeting, I found out that we should gear up for a new boss: Marvin Davis, the billionaire oilman from Denver. So began the dawn of a new regime at Fox.

Standing at six feet four inches and weighing over three hundred pounds, Marvin Davis was a larger-than-life figure who swallowed everything in front of him—food, people, you name it. If you had to sum up his vocation in one word, it would be *trading*, but Marvin's financial life was murkier than a Florida swamp. Once ranked by *Forbes* as the thirtieth-richest man in America with a net worth of $5.8 billion, his eldest daughter has alleged that he died broke and that his wealth was greatly exaggerated. While the jury's still out on how much money he lost over the course of his lifetime, he certainly made billions.

Amid my chaotic employment status, I had no idea whether Marvin was an ally or an enemy. Unbeknownst to Stanfill, Marvin flew me to his office in Denver to discuss my future with the company. I'd seen a lot of big offices by then, but nothing like Marvin's. It had a sprawling hallway leading up to his workspace, and his desk stood upon a platform so that he looked down upon his visitors. Not that Marvin needed a booster seat; he towered over everyone he encountered. After a few minutes of boilerplate chitchat, Marvin gave me a vague indication that he was on my side.

"Be patient, Harris. Go home and do your job."

In the weeks that followed, Marvin Davis pulled a snow job on Dennis Stanfill like I had never seen. In addition to putting $7 million into Stanfill's pocket based on shares alone, Marvin promised Dennis that he would remain the controlling executive at the studio. After a parade of social extravagances, Dennis was convinced that Marvin was loyal to him. The board prepared the paperwork, and with the scribble of Marvin's ham-size hand, Fox became a private company.

About a month after Marvin's purchase of Fox, Stanfill flew to his office to deliver the coup de grâce to yours truly. Of course I wasn't in the room, so I'm speaking on account of Marvin's testimony. Dennis allegedly laid down firm terms—it was either him or me. One executive would remain at Fox, and the other would have to leave. Stanfill supposedly rose out of his chair and headed for the door.

"Dennis," Marvin called from behind his desk. "Did you fly to Denver in the Fox jet?" Dennis turned and nodded. "Fly home commercial— you're no longer with the company."

Marvin Davis didn't like being harangued or told what to do. He also couldn't stand Dennis Stanfill, coining him a member of the "gentile mafia." From the very first dinner he had with Stanfill, he was plotting to shoulder him out of power. As for defending me, Marvin called Lew Wasserman to get a sense of my moral standards, and Lew had lain out in traffic for me. I later learned that a squadron of heavy hitters had echoed Lew, including CAA co-founders Michael Ovitz and Bill Haber, along with power attorneys Skip Brittenham and Kenny Ziffren. It's impossible to avoid nemeses in the entertainment industry. That means you better find some friends who will protect you during crunch time. Otherwise, you'll have a very short career.

The press blew up like Mount Vesuvius when Fox's PR department released the news of Stanfill's departure. No one had seen it coming— remember, Marvin and Stanfill had been palling around Los Angeles for the past month like newlyweds. In the wake of the announcement, I returned to a piece of advice that Lew Wasserman gave me after I lost a client at MCA.

"Don't get mad," Lew had said calmly. "Get even."

Grinning, I called the head of security at Fox.

"Would you please escort Chuck Weiss off the lot?" I've been lucky enough to experience a few fleeting moments of pure redemption throughout the course of my career. One of them was watching the Fox guards throw Chuck Weiss's ass on the curb.

Later that week, Fox threw a party to celebrate the ousting of our prickly CEO. Someone bought a cake with Stanfill's face screened onto the sinking *Titanic*. But as we all rejoiced, everyone in senior management was thinking the same thing. Behind the jovial three-hundred-pound frame, who was Marvin Davis?

The pen may be mightier than the sword, but gossip is a hand grenade. It's astounding to think about how much power gossip holds over Hollywood. Among the *National Enquirer*, TMZ, and the countless blogs that seek out baby bumps and nipple slips, we're all slaves to rumor. After all, who doesn't want a secret window into the life of an A-list celebrity? Gossip, as destructive as it is, breaks down the artificial wall of exclusivity and makes Joe and Jane Public feel like they're in the know. The problem is that most of it isn't true.

While the consequences of gossip might feel superficial, I believe that it's a major reason why the entertainment industry has been plagued by a history of heinous behaviors carried out by power-wielding moguls. How, for instance, did a fellow like Harvey Weinstein get away with decades of sexual abuse? I can assure you that everyone in Hollywood—executives, creatives, assistants—had heard *something* of Harvey's monstrous tendencies. So why didn't they surface earlier? Sure, a major component involved his power in the industry. But just as importantly, Harvey got away with his ploys because *no one knew if they were true*. Gossip diluted the crimes that he carried out on a consistent basis. The same dynamic applies to other guilty titans in show business: Bill Cosby, Brett Ratner, and countless other men who leveraged their status against unassuming victims. Although skewing the truth might make for a better story, we need to check our flapping gums every once in a while. We owe it to the industry.

An Oilman Meets a Media Mogul
1980-1986

Marvin Davis was an oilman who liked to play. After graduating from New York University, he got his start in the Texas fracking business. He fashioned himself an independent driller, searching for oceans of thick, black liquid beneath the Midwestern crust. In other words, he was a gambler. His success derived from luck, which he deemed intuition. Whatever you want to call it, he accrued 767,000 acres of exploratory land and 830 oil wells.

Marvin had always been infatuated with Hollywood. Ever since his wedding at the Beverly Hills Hotel, he'd been looking for a way to enter the world of entertainment, but he learned that film producers tend to steer clear of southern oil moguls. If Marvin was going to make it into the business, he was going to have to buy his way in. During the heat of Dennis Stanfill's bogus investigation against me, he got his chance. Marvin was approached by the CEO of Hiram Walker and its oil production subsidiary, Home Oil Company, with interest in purchasing Marvin's empire. Despite his wells being 20 to 25 percent below reported levels, Marvin made out of the deal with $630 million. That sale enabled him to purchase Fox for a figure of $720 million. What no one knew was that Marvin only put up half of that money. He had an invisible partner: the commodities trader Marc Rich.

If that name rings a bell, it's because Marc became famous for evading $48 million in taxes and making oil deals with Iran during the Iran hostage crisis. He also made a dark blot on Bill Clinton's administration when he received a controversial pardon from the president on his last day in office. To this day, critics remain adamant that the pardon was a function of Marc's numerous financial gifts to the Clinton Foundation.

Before the world found out he was a crook, Marc and his partner Pincus "Pinky" Green contacted Marvin to invest in the oil business. Marvin knew that Marc and Pinky had exorbitant sums of money, and when he resolved to buy Fox, he figured that a secret partnership would mitigate his own financial risk. By then, Marc was into some fishy business and had no interest holding voting power in the company. He agreed to front 50 percent of the purchase price on the condition that Marvin immediately liquidate Fox's assets, which included the Pebble Beach Golf Course, the Aspen Skiing Corporation, Coca-Cola bottling plants across the Midwest, and the Hoyts movie theaters in Australia and New Zealand. The arrangement suited Marvin well; he got to be the face of the operation while recouping his investment by auctioning off Fox's portfolio. He got a little scissor-happy at one point, allegedly making a handshake deal with Kirk Kerkorian to sell Fox's movie and television divisions. That transaction would have reduced Fox to a mere carcass, but it never went through. Despite Marvin's gaudy displays of excess, his life was all smoke and mirrors. He was the stingiest spendthrift I ever encountered, who cared far more for appearance than the company's long-term finances.

Amid Marvin's liquidation campaign, Marc got pinched on sixty-five criminal counts of tax evasion, wire fraud, racketeering, and of course trading with Iran while it held US hostages. Desperate, Marc loaded up a Swiss airplane with damning documents, but the feds grounded it before it could take off from the John F. Kennedy International Airport in New York. Marc fled to Switzerland and spent the next eighteen years on the FBI's ten most wanted fugitives list. In fact, years later while staying at the Berkeley Hotel in London, I encountered the spitting image of Marc Rich sitting at the bar. I wasn't positive it was him until he lit up one of his cheap, greasy cigars. I never could figure out why a billionaire smoked such garbage. Anyways, thirty feet before I could pat him on the back, three men the size of my house grabbed me by the armpits and shuffled me out of the bar.

"Don't make me call Scotland Yard," I growled at them. But there was no need for a scuffle—Marc called them off and we had a drink at the bar.

"Who are those guys?" I asked him.

"Mossad warriors, courtesy of the Israeli government. I've been very generous to some senior officials over there."

That was the last time I ever saw Marc Rich.

Marvin was thrilled when he heard about Marc's indictment—he had one less bird chirping in his ear. More, he made out like a bandit buying Marc's half of the company from the US Justice Department for just $116 million.

I remember Marvin Davis's first meeting at Fox after he bought the studio. He had plans to acquaint himself with every senior executive, but he made a bit of a blunder when he met Sherry Lansing.

"Could you get me two cups of coffee, dear?" he asked when she entered.

"Oh. I'm Sherry Lansing. I run the film department."

"I'm looking for Jerry Lansing," Marvin responded.

"There is no Jerry Lansing. I'm Sherry."

Marvin was one of the few people who could shrug off that type of faux pas without blushing. You know how you can envision the exact portrait of some people as five-year-olds on a kindergarten playground? That was Marvin every day. He was a three-hundred-pound kid with billions to spend on toys.

Under Marvin's thumb, Fox was a platform for excess and showmanship. Every month, he assembled the Fox board for a grand dinner at the hottest restaurant of the time. In addition to myself, Alan Hirschfield, Sherry Lansing, and Norman Levy, the board included public figures like Henry Kissinger and former president Gerald Ford. The meals were the closest you could get to King Louis XIV's feasts at Versailles. Marvin's ravenous appetite led to him scarfing down a lobster and a steak in one sitting, and he assumed that everyone consumed a similar volume. On one occasion, I hired three off-duty firemen to burst into the restaurant halfway through the meal. Lugging in oxygen tanks and vials of Pepto-Bismol, they marched straight up to Marvin.

"Harris hired us to revive you when you go into cardiac arrest," one of them said. Marvin rewarded my practical joke with an invitation to invest in his oil business.

"I can guarantee an 8 percent return," Marvin shouted triumphantly at the senior executives. Everyone agreed to throw $200,000 in the pot, except for Sherry Lansing who was more fiscally responsible than anyone else. A few months later, Alan Hirschfield rang me.

"Are you sitting down?" he asked.

"Sure am."

"Marvin Davis outsmarted himself. He threw our money at an oil field in Wyoming, and it hit a wildcat!"

"What the hell's a wildcat?" I asked.

As it turned out, we hit an oil geyser as steady as Old Faithful. For months, I got checks for $60,000—I was making more money in the oil business than I was as president of Fox Television. When Marvin returned for a new round of investments, everyone went in—including Sherry Lansing, John Ritter, and George Lucas. This time I tossed $250,000 into the pot, but we hit twelve dry wells and lost our return.

Greed is everyone's kryptonite.

There were a lot of things to learn from Marvin Davis, much of which involved how not to act. He couldn't help himself from pushing the envelope a bit too far on every transaction he made. Marvin's insatiable thirst for fun proved to be infectious; I found myself at my most reckless under his regime. Despite the glitz of Hollywood, it's important to stay humble and sober regardless of the people surrounding you.

As dangerous as I found Marvin's appetite for showmanship, I did enjoy rubbing elbows with some of his top figures on the Fox board. I developed a close friendship with former US president Gerald Ford on the golf course at Pebble Beach. For as far as he'd gotten in politics, he had a truly atrocious swing. In fact, he nearly decapitated five onlookers on a wild slice off the tee. In one of our board meetings, Gerald brought up the upcoming Republican National Convention, where Ronald Reagan would ultimately receive the party's endorsement. Ford was used to speaking in front of Congress, but he wasn't quite sure of what to say in a pep-rally environment. The two of us ended up workshopping his speech, an honor that I still revere to this day.

Luckily for me, Marvin decided to hold on to Aspen. That meant I could continue my tradition of spending Christmas and New Year's on the slopes free of charge. Marvin had his own private aircraft, so the Fox jet was mine for the taking. One holiday season, the pilot noted that a major blizzard was rolling in on New Year's Eve. He suggested we flee Aspen before all hell broke loose. It turned out that every heavy hitter in Aspen had a similar idea—when we got to the airport, I found all the head honchos grumbling in the terminals. Though the airport had already suspended all outbound flights, incoming planes were still permitted to land. Of course, no one in their right mind would do so—God knew how long the blizzard would last. I, along with the rest of the vacationing Hollywood executives, marveled at a plane descending onto the airway. I squinted to find the San Diego Chargers' logo on the tail wing. Moments later, a fussy woman with four poodles strolled into the terminal. She was the wife of Alex Spanos, the owner of the Chargers. He had intended to drop off Mrs. Spanos to ski before continuing to a home game in sunny Southern California. Little did he know that once his wheels hit the tarmac, he was stuck. From where I sat, I could hear his pilot communicating with the control tower.

"Requesting takeoff," the pilot said.

"All flights are grounded. You're last in line to leave."

"How long would you estimate the delay?"

"A few days."

"Mr. Spanos has a game in San Diego tomorrow. Can we make an exception?" The control tower started to chuckle.

"We suggest that Mr. Spanos get a car."

The Fox jet was next in line to leave, and for a moment I contemplated giving my spot to Spanos. Then I remembered that I was a fan of the Los Angeles Raiders. Moments later, I was approached by Michael Eisner, the sitting CEO of Disney.

"I need your help, Harris—I have an important meeting tomorrow. Can we swap?"

"I checked out of my hotel. If you can find a place for me to sleep tonight, it's all yours."

"Stay in my cabin—it's fully staffed."

So I let Michael Eisner take my spot and planned to leave Aspen the following day. I would find that Eisner uses the term *cabin* rather loosely—his place was more like a palatial mansion.

"Who are you meeting with, anyhow?" I asked before he took off.

"The governor of Florida. He wants to speak about new attractions at Disney World."

Eight years later, *The Lion King* opened on Broadway to spectacular reviews. It was the *Hamilton* of the '90s, and my family happened to be in New York the week it opened. I lobbed a call into Michael Eisner.

"Could I get eight tickets to your play?" I asked.

"It's sold out for a year," Eisner answered.

"Remember Aspen?" Eight lucky Katlemans got the best seats in the house that week.

Keep track of your favors.

In a collaborative business like entertainment, IOUs are the most precious currency. That being said—and I hate to sound like a heartless executive—there isn't any such thing as a genuine favor in Hollywood. It doesn't matter how many times someone fills your glass or tells you they have your back. . . everyone wants something, and acts of charity don't exist. The quality of the favors you receive are directly determined by the extent to which others think you can benefit them in the future. It may sound sleazy, but you get what you sign up for.

Even when dealing with a trusted friend or colleague, I would caution young executives to cash in favors as a last resort. That doesn't mean to never ask for help; there will be times when you need someone's influence to get you out of a jam. But if you ask someone to lay out for you, you better be ready to do the same for them whenever they call.

That is, of course, unless you need tickets to a top-rate play on Broadway.

For all the fun I had at Fox, there was a lot of work to be done if I wanted to turn the television department around. Fox's new owner could barely recite the three television networks of the time, which put the onus of our performance entirely on me.

As I've mentioned, I hedged my career philosophy on the value of storytellers over actors. The most coveted executive producer at the time was Glen A. Larson, who was responsible for legendary television series like *It Takes a Thief*, *The Virginian*, *The Hardy Boys*, *Battlestar Galatica*, *The Six Million Dollar Man*, and *Magnum, P.I.* He happened to be represented by the attorney Skip Brittenham, who drafted my deal at Fox. Skip and I had a longtime friendship that I endeavored to use to my advantage.

"If you can get me in the room with Glen Larson, I'll give you and his attorneys a 5 percent packaging fee when I sign him," I promised. Skip agreed and set the meeting.

"If you want Glen to leave the studio that's made him famous, you better have a juicy bone for him to gnaw on," he said.

Skip was right; Universal Television had more shows on the air than all the other studios combined. Leaving that place was like fleeing the archdiocese. Before my meeting with Glen, I called upon my training from Lew Wasserman. I remembered that dinner at Chasen's with Clark Gable; Lew had known exactly how much Clark was getting paid, and he used his deal terms to present an offer that couldn't be denied. I resolved to do the same thing with Glen.

Glen's arrangement at UTV was based on a theoretical profit percentage. That meant that realistically, he never saw any money from syndication or reruns. In fact, the studio treated him like a salaried employee. I offered Glen an unprecedented arrangement: a modified gross deal that surrendered a percentage of ownership to Glen himself. That meant that if Glen brought a series in on budget, he would see profits on foreign sales during the first year of airing. He'd see domestic profits in the second year if the network renewed the series.

Glen didn't have much of a choice; he thanked Frank Price, the chairman of UTV, and signed with me. Glen pulled in over $100 million for the studio. Just as valuable was the message that we sent to the town by signing him. For the first time in decades, Fox Television was for real. That being said, not all of Glen's shows were hits, per se. I remember him knocking on my door with an idea that had him jazzed.

"It's a hard-boiled genre show that follows a guy who fights crime."

"Sounds like every show I've ever seen," I responded.

"No, it doesn't. This guy doesn't use weapons. He gets the bad guys by transforming into any animal he wants. I call it. . . *Manimal*."

"Glen, I wouldn't tell you this if I didn't think you were a genius. That might be the dumbest idea I've ever heard. Go back to the drawing board."

But the idea of a man morphing into a house cat or what have you had infected Glen, and he started pitching the concept to executives around town. When the NBC tastemaker Brandon Tartikoff jumped on the idea, the project started to roll forward like a train without brakes. NBC hired a sweaty-palmed writer called Donald Boyle, and Tartikoff gave Glen a massive budget. That was like to giving an AK-47 to a serial killer.

"NBC better cover the deficits," I told Tartikoff, "because this is going to be a nightmare."

Manimal was one of the biggest television fiascos of its era, broadcasting for only seven episodes before getting canceled for terrible ratings. The critics hated it even more than the public did. Months later, when Brandon Tartikoff was featured on *Saturday Night Live*, he turned to the camera and apologized.

"My good friend Harris Katleman convinced me to green-light *Manimal*. He was incredulous."

Needless to say, he found that joke funnier than I did. Looking back, I suppose *Manimal* was ahead of its time. Look at movies like *Wolfman*, *Harry Potter*, and anything that Rob Schneider has ever done. Animal transformations happen all the time—Glen was just too early to the party.

Glen's biggest hit was *The Fall Guy*, an action-drama about a stuntman who moonlights as a bounty hunter. The star was Lee Majors, whose list of credits is longer than Beldon Katleman's list of enemies. At the craft service cart, Lee boasted about how much money his bookie had made for him through sports betting. By this point, the El Rancho had long burned to a crisp and we Katlemans had lost our Vegas connections. In other words, I was in the market for a bookie.

"The guy's name is Norm the Iceman," Lee told me.

I placed a number of bets with Norm, but I wasn't as lucky as Lee. By the end of the season, I had lost somewhere around $1,000, and the Iceman wanted to collect.

"Should I drive to his office?" my assistant asked.

"Why don't you hold off for now," I said. I didn't let on any concern, but with a name like that, I was convinced that Norm the Iceman was an assassin.

At the end of the lunch hour, my assistant came down the hallway clutching a bucket of Baskin-Robbins ice cream.

"What a lovely man Norm is. He gave me two gallons of rocky road on the house!" So much for me thinking he was related to Vito Corleone. It turns out that he owned two Baskin-Robbins ice cream stores.

Glen was just the start of my division's relationships with top writers. Over the years to come, I dedicated my efforts to signing Hollywood's greatest talents to the studio. That included Suzanne Pleshette, Richard and Esther Shapiro, James Henerson and James Hirsch, Paul Junger Witt and Tony Thomas, Clyde B. Phillips, Marc Merson, Bob Schiller and Bob Weiskopf, Steven Bochco, and James L. Brooks.

The creators are your only assets.

When you're running a television studio, you aren't drumming up story concepts or penning any scripts. Neither are you dealing with the nuts and bolts of production, and you sure as hell don't know how to operate a camera. Your chief value, then, involves the creative minds that you sign to your brand. At the end of the day, it's pretty simple: if you sign A-plus creators, you'll make at least a few hits. If you sign a bunch of hacks, you'll crash and burn. My ability to succeed at Fox didn't involve any raw talents of my own. Rather, it boiled down to signing the right creatives at the right time and fostering a culture that encouraged premium content.

Even with all the new talent at Fox, Marvin Davis mandated that he needed extra dough out of the studio. What else was new? Anyone with the business sense of a fifth grader could see we had a tremendous profit center in the *Star Wars* movies, each of which were owned by Fox. The box office profits were already in the bank, but we had yet to license the franchise to air on network television. Remember, I'd facilitated the licensing of three hundred MGM titles in ten days, so I figured that I could make a killer deal. When I reviewed the contracts, however, I noticed that all licensing transactions had to be signed off by the grandfather of *Star Wars* himself: George Lucas.

I flew up to Skywalker Ranch, George's forty-seven-hundred-acre headquarters nestled in the rolling hills of Marin County. The Victorian-style house included a sprawling screening room, a domed research library, and a state-of-the-art pool. George had even built a lake on the property, which he dubbed Lake Ewok.

When I sat with George, he made it clear that he wasn't going to approve just any licensing deal.

"I'll only permit a transaction north of $15 million."

If you're George Lucas and you create something as iconic as *Star Wars*, you want to protect the brand. The only thing worse than letting his legacy fall victim to endless reruns would be putting Episodes I, II, and III in the hands of Jar Jar Binks. But $15 million is a lot of money. I returned to Los Angeles with my work cut out for me.

You might be wondering how the licensing of an old movie could hold such value. The answer is advertising. If you're the only channel that broadcasts *Star Wars*, the entire world will tune in. Advertisers pay networks more money than you could fathom for marquee commercial time. The public views television as shows separated by commercials, whereas the industry views television as commercials separated by shows.

After leveraging all the networks against one another, I got CBS up to $22 million for just three airings. After those broadcasts, the rights would revert back to Fox, and we could renegotiate another licensing deal if we felt like it. I was fairly confident that I could wring another million or two out of CBS, but it would certainly ruffle some feathers at the network. I decided to broach the dilemma with Marvin.

"Close the deal," Marvin said. "Let's let the other side think they've won."

Leave a few scraps on the table.

I figured that hell would freeze over before Marvin Davis took a moderate business position, but he proved me wrong. Closing the CBS deal at $22 million strengthened my relationship with the network. And when I told George Lucas that I had overshot his demand by $7 million, he was over the moon.

Thinking back on things, my philosophy in licensing *Star Wars* contradicted my take-no-prisoners approach to licensing MGM's crown jewels. It all depends on the context, as well as your marching orders. While Kirk Kerkorian needed to generate cash to pump into his casinos, Marvin Davis's principal interest involved schmoozing and socializing. In other words, he wanted to avoid having the majority of Hollywood hate his guts.

To keep my stable of storytellers happy, I renewed a practice that I'd started as president of MGM. Each week, I devoted a few hours to mingling with the lot's actors, directors, and production workers so I wouldn't come across as a suit sitting in an ivory tower. It's easy to forget about the gritty production details, but at the end of the day the real magic of the business happens on the soundstages.

One afternoon, I visited the set of *Trapper John, M.D.*, one of the two shows that I inherited from Russ Barry. As the grips were lighting a new set piece, I started chatting with the actor Greg Harrison, one of the show's leading men.

"It seems to me that there's more turnover in the deal-making world than there is in talent," he said. "And that's saying a lot."

"There's a premium on capable people," I replied.

"I know a guy who would blow you away," said Greg. "He's wants to be an actor, but he's too smart to make it in front of the camera. He should be controlling a studio."

"What does he do?"

"He's a bartender at the Hollywood Improv. His wife tries to book him guest-starring gigs, but they're few and far between."

"What's his name?" I asked.

"Les Moonves."

The following week, I found myself staring down the future CEO of CBS in my office. If you surround yourself with actors for long enough, you can sniff out their musk a mile away, and Les was no exception. He had a movie-star smile and a social ease about him. It seemed he was just as comfortable in my office as I was. But unlike most of the actors whom I had encountered, Les knew everything there was to know about the film and television business. I would have guessed he'd spent a few years in the trenches of an agency, but Les had merely picked things up on the fly. Before he left, I handed him the first draft of a pilot that had just been submitted to the studio.

"Give it a read, and let me know what you think."

When I got into my office the next morning, Les's comments were waiting in my inbox.

"Jesus," I said to myself as I scanned the page. "These are better than what my staff came up with."

When you find a guy with social grace, sharp intellect, and an understanding of story, you scoop him up. I offered Les a position in my movie of the week department, and Les gave his two-week notice at the Improv.

Six months into the job, the head of Les's department, Dick Rosetti, fell ill.

"Congratulations," I told Les. "You're the department head."

"I don't know how to run a department," Les said.

"I didn't know how to run a studio when Kirk Kerkorian hired me, and Kirk Kerkorian didn't know how to be a CEO when he bought MGM. You'll either figure it out or you won't."

Les did the former. Under his leadership, the department's profits skyrocketed. Movies of the week, however, lacked the panache that the Fox board was chasing. Six months after Les's promotion, I received executive orders to shut it down.

Though he was one of the youngest executives working for me, I thought that Les was one of the most talented. But there wasn't any room for him in television. So I called in my head of development, Peter Grad, and broached the possibility of swapping Les for the man working directly beneath him.

"We can't risk losing Les to another studio," I told Peter. "That's not a guy you want working against you." But Peter was adamant on protecting his guy.

"You're the one I learned loyalty from, boss."

As my second attempt to keep Les around, I tried to ease him into Fox's motion picture department, which was being run by Scott Rudin. Since leaving Fox, Rudin has produced Hollywood's best films: every Coen brothers project, all of Wes Anderson's work, you name it. Les swung by my office directly after his interview with Scott.

"Don't think it could have gone any better," he said optimistically. Later that afternoon, Rudin phoned me.

"I'm not gonna hire your guy."

"Why not?"

"He'll dislodge me."

With back-to-back efforts foiled, I was still delaying Barry's mandate to shut down Fox's movie of the week department, and he was getting pissed.

"If you don't have the stones to kill it, then I will!" I remember him yelling at me. With my back against the wall, I picked up my phone and called Merv Adelson, the president and cofounder of Lorimar. The Adelsons and Katlemans had moved to California from Nebraska together, and Merv and I had grown close over the years. I knew he needed a top-notch development guy, and he leaped on Les as a new hire. I got a call from Barry Diller minutes after Les tendered his resignation.

"How'd we let him get away?"

"For starters, we shut down his department," I replied.

Four years later, Warner Bros. bought Lorimar, which paved the way for Les to become president and CEO of Warner Bros. Television. There, he green-lit *Friends* and *ER*, which all but entranced audiences in the '90s. Les didn't stop at running the most successful television studio in town—in 1995, he joined CBS Entertainment, where he ultimately rose to become chairman and CEO. This position granted Les control not only of CBS's massive platform, but of a broad portfolio of companies including the premium cable channel Showtime, the broadcast network The CW, the publishing powerhouse Simon & Schuster, and the streaming platform CBS All Access. Les's reach has allowed him to shepherd programs including *60 Minutes*, *The Big Bang Theory*, *Survivor*, and *CSI*, among a laundry list of others. Chances are that if you've ever gotten sucked into a television show, it probably has Les's fingerprints on it.

Keep your eyes peeled for the messiah.

The hierarchy of entertainment means there will always be a person at the top, and there will always be a person on the rise. If you're looking to be a rainmaker, you need to keep an eye out for the next figure who's going to change the business. For me, that was Leslie Moonves. As a bartender with minimal experience in boardrooms, Les was far from the obvious hire. But when you're looking to build a team, an applicant's potential outweighs his or her past experiences. Every mogul slaved away at a menial job at one point—that doesn't stunt the ability to lead. In a business in which you never know who's going to make it to the top, it's best to consider every newcomer with fresh eyes and respect. That way they won't fire you if they become your boss down the line.

A quick note about Les in the wake of the *New Yorker* exposé. The article discusses the accounts of six women who have accused Les of sexual assault throughout his illustrious career. I was floored while reading the article, as I never saw evidence of this sort of behavior. I can only chime in on Les's uncanny business prowess and his friendship to me. I'll leave the other matters to the people who have authority to speak: the investigators and the brave women who have come forward.

Just because I had to compete against Les when he left Fox didn't mean I stopped seeing him on a regular basis. The two of us were involved in a weekly, high-stakes poker game on Thursday nights. Gary Nardino, the president of Paramount Television, hosted the contest at his house in Beverly Hills. We had dinner catered in every week at 6:00 p.m., and by 7:30 p.m. we were guarding $5,000 worth of chips as Gary dealt the cards. We had one rule on which we all agreed: no business talk.

In addition to me, Les, and Gary, the following members were in attendance every week: Bob Broder, co-founder of ICM Partners; Bill Haber, co-founder of CAA; Michael Zinberg, the Texan television director; John McMahon, head of NBC programming; Larry Gordon, producer of *Die Hard*; and Michael Eisner, CEO of Disney. The fill-in players were the famous restaurateur Dan Tana, Johnny Carson, and Barry Diller. The only civilian among the group was Jerry Steiner, the current head of the breast cancer unit at Cedars-Sinai Hospital. One evening, I remember Jerry's phone ringing in the middle of a hand.

"Shouldn't you grab that?" one of us asked. We knew that Jerry was on call. Jerry reluctantly fumbled for his phone.

"Really?" he said into the speaker. "Oh. Is the family on their way? Okay, got it." He hung up the phone and fanned his cards.

"Do you have to run?" I asked.

"Not yet. Patient is terminally ill, but the family lives in Santa Barbara. I have another hour before I have to leave."

That earned Jerry the nickname of "Action Doc," as he could never keep his hands out of the game. He was a consistent loser.

Jerry wasn't a card shark, but the real caboose of the bunch was Dan Tana. Every week, he would lose buckets of money, to the point where the group started feeling bad. One week, the players elected me to dissuade Tana from continuing his suffering. I wasn't looking forward to it;

with a career playing professional soccer in Yugoslavia and Belgium, Tana had a competitive streak. I took him out to lunch one day and broached the topic.

"Dan—you know we love you and want you around for dinner, but you're overmatched at the card table."

"Fuck you!" Tana roared. "I can afford to lose double what I'm losing now. I want to keep playing." So much for not shooting the messenger. Dan Tana remained a fixture in the game, and the rest of us continued raking in his chips.

Though we never played with Kirk Kerkorian or Marvin Davis-level money, the stakes of our game were high enough to boil blood. Mind you, as a collection of Hollywood executives and moguls, we were a rather scrappy bunch. I remember Michael Eisner taking an inordinate amount of time to make a decision with his hand. In his Texan accent, Michael Zinberg broke the silence.

"Why don't you ask Barry Diller what to do?"

Eisner threw his cards down on the table and nearly ripped Zinberg's throat out. That was the last time that Eisner ever graced the poker table.

Just after an awards season, Les broke the cardinal rule of the game. Though Warner Bros. Television had more series on the air, my shows consistently raked in awards.

"How the fuck do you get a Golden Globe in this town?"

"I'll tell you when I leave Fox."

Fast-forward several years, when I was a free man beyond the clutches of the studio. Les and I met for lunch.

"The jig's up. God knows your shows weren't that much better than mine. How did you get all those Golden Globes?"

"You know how the Globes are determined?" I fired back.

"The Foreign Press."

"Yeah, exactly. And they're a bunch of freeloaders who don't have a free dollar to spend. Every awards season, I threw them a bottomless lunch at the hottest restaurant in town. They returned the favor with votes."

Nothing sweetens the deal like the crab louie at the Grill. With the amount of awards Les has won since then, I'd be surprised if he didn't adopt my scheme.

📺

Anyone who's ever worked in the heart of a major studio understands that power transfers more frequently than it did during the French Revolution. To put it simply, Hollywood's a risky business that doesn't accept mistakes. Every boss is fickle, and every executive is dispensable once his or her numbers begin to wilt. All of these factors exert pressure upon an executive, which inspires the boardroom tirades for which Hollywood is famous. No one knows those better than Jonathan Dolgen, the top dog in Fox's film finance division, who went on to become the chairman of the Viacom Entertainment Group. Jonathan scared the hell out of most people on account of mere appearance. With eyes like a specter and a bullet-size gap between his front two teeth, Jonathan had a look that could make you stop dead in your tracks. Jonathan smoked about ten packs of cigarettes and drank a pot of black coffee every day.

I remember sitting in Jonathan's office when his lead accountant delivered him some data that didn't gel with him. He grabbed an office chair by its arm and flung it at his window, which shattered into innumerable pieces. Luckily his office was on the first floor and no passing civilians were impaled by glass shards. The accountant looked as if he had just witnessed a cat being skinned, and I burst out laughing.

"What the fuck are you laughing about?!" Dolgen screamed.

"It's seven o'clock on a Friday night, and you're too paranoid to leave the office with an open window. You're gonna be here all night."

You see, Jonathan had everything short of the nuclear codes in his office files, and there was no chance he'd risk a custodian or curious assistant stepping in for a peek. He ended up waiting in that office until two in the morning until someone could replace the window.

Jonathan lost his cool more often than necessary, but I understood where he was coming from. The head of a studio needs to know how to manage people, and sometimes that means putting the fear of God into brewing mutineers.

I had minted Bobby Morin as my vice president of syndication the month I arrived at Fox. I met Bobby at MGM, where we worked together until Frank Rosenfelt fired him. Rosenfelt, along with the bulk of Hollywood, thought that Bobby was a snake. I didn't necessarily disagree, but I would tell people that he was *my* snake. Plus, I needed a spitfire in syndication, and Bobby knew how to sell shows.

Fast-forward a few years when I'd just returned from a tedious business trip in Europe. Alan Hirschfield had me take a seat in his office.

"Your guy Robert Morin thinks he can do your job better than you can," Alan said.

"Says who?"

"Says Morin. He came into my office while you were gone to suggest I fire you and promote him. I suggest you get your team in order."

It took restraint to walk out of Alan's office without flipping the desk over. Forget the betrayal: to go whining to Alan once I left the country? If you're going to be manipulative, you better have tact. Bobby obviously had none. I told my assistant that I didn't care if Bobby was speaking to the president; he better be in my office within five minutes.

You know when a dog looks at you after peeing in the house? You can smell the guilt on him. That's what Bobby looked like as he entered my office. He knew he was fucked.

"I've been spending the better part of an hour thinking about what I should do to you, Bobby. I can't kill you, because I don't have those connections. I could beat the living shit out of you, but that would be too easy."

Bobby's eyes started welling with tears.

"Harris, I thought we could do it together—"

"Do it together?!" I asked. "Your wife made me dinner; I gave you your job... this is how you return the favor?" Now I was on the other side of my desk, centimeters away from his face. Bobby started blubbering like a fool. I'll stop there and leave the rest of my tirade to the imagination. Minutes later, I was seated again.

"I've made up my mind. I'm going to torture you, Bobby. You know the bonus you're supposed to get in three months?"

Bobby nodded.

"I'm giving it to the Jewish welfare. Now, I know that violates your contract, and I know that everyone around here lives off their bonuses. So I guess you have three options. You can sue, you can leave, or you can do your job until your contract expires."

That was the last time Bobby Morin tried to cut in line. I got two years of exemplary work out of him before his contract was up.

On another occasion, I remember finding out that one of my executives was having an affair with a co-worker from Fox Merchandising. When he cut things off and the mistress sued him for sexual harassment, he approached me with his tail between his legs. He needed $250,000 to cover the settlement. I considered this man a close friend, but I couldn't cover up the situation without involving corporate accounting. More, I had learned from Dennis Stanfill that scandals can blow up for much less. I didn't want to expose myself to any shady business. After deliberating with my superiors, I called the executive into my office.

"I have good news and bad news. Good news is that we'll pay the settlement. Bad news is that every cent comes out of your paycheck." The color drained from his face.

"But my wife gets the paychecks. What am I gonna tell her when she finds a quarter million dollars missing?"

"Tell her you put your cock in the wrong pussy."

There were instances in which I had to bring the hammer down upon my entire team. I wasn't as hardcore as Barry Diller, but if you let employees get too comfortable, they'll start dragging their toes. At the end of each selling season, Fox treated the high-level executives to an all-expenses-paid vacation wherever we wanted to go. That gave my staff reason to sing a merry tune come August. But one abysmal year, we sold just two of the nine pilots we shot. That's worse than Shaquille O'Neal's free-throw percentage. I called my staff into the boardroom where we traditionally chose a vacation spot.

"I don't think I need to tell you how embarrassing this year has been," I stated. The room nodded sullenly. "So why don't we skip ahead to vacation planning? We've all earned it, haven't we?"

You could have snapped the air with a pair of blunt scissors.

"Rather than opening it up to a vote, I've preemptively made arrangements for all eighteen of us. All the rooms in Death Valley were booked, so we're going to Palm Springs. The average high is expected to be 112 degrees. Hopefully you'll learn how much I sweat to get where I am today."

I remember Peter Grad's golf tee melting into the asphalt when he knelt down to tie his shoe. When we went eight for eight the next selling season, my staff and I spent a week in Hawaii.

Know when to use the whip.

In his Cadillac on the way to Hollywood Park, I remember Lew Wasserman telling me that there are three types of racehorses. First, you have the nervy types that break from the starting gate like terrified antelopes. You can't touch these ones with the whip or they'll fall to pieces—they're too delicate. Then you have your moderately tempered horse. These ones break clean, but in the home stretch they need a little tap on the rump. And finally, you have the stubborn thoroughbreds. They might have God-given speed, but in order to get a good race out of them, the jockey needs to give them a proper spanking. I'm not one for animal cruelty, but the same logic applies to leading a team of executives. If you're trying to get the best performance out of your staff, you can't treat each person the same. You have to understand the way their brains work and manage them accordingly. Peter Grad galloped through the finish line without any welts on his rump. Robert Morin needed to be spanked.

I never enjoyed punishing my staff. But if you have the good fortune of attaining power and you want to keep it, there comes a time when you have to chew someone out. If you're not comfortable getting in someone's face, you're not cut out to lead. The key is to make sure there's always an end goal to your disciplinary measure. It's easy to get caught up in a yelling bout—especially when an underling has been digging your grave—but at the end of the day, you have to remember that nothing's personal in business. Leaders are obliged to build someone back up just as much as they break a person down. After blowing out my voice box with one of the most epic ass chewings in Fox's storied history, I could have told Robert Morin that his career was over. But by giving him the opportunity to keep his job, I was able to sustain a solid working environment until the end of his contract. All employees need to feel hope for their future—that there's a light they can chase at their company.

One of the programs that pushed our division into the green was *Mr. Belvedere*, my beloved pest of a show. I'd been taken by a cluster of movies—*Mr. Belvedere Goes to College, Mr. Belvedere Rings the Bell*—starring Clifton Webb. The title character was an effete British butler who had been hired by a ragtag American family. The films stirred something in me—I could see that character thriving on the television screen. I floated the idea past Frank Dungan and Jeff Stein—two comedy writers whom I had signed to Fox—who gravitated to the concept and went straight to work. A few months later, we sold the pilot to ABC and dived into the casting process. We pinned down most of the roles rather quickly, but our casting department couldn't find anyone who fit the bill for the father of the family.

"We're at an impasse," said the casting sage Lynn Stalmaster. I spent a week racking my brain for a reasonable prototype. I found the guy on my television screen as I watched *The Johnny Carson Show* before bed. Bob Uecker, dubbed Mr. Baseball by Johnny Carson himself, was one of the most common guests on the talk show. He was Jimmy Fallon's Justin Timberlake, David Letterman's Bill Murray—except not an actor. An announcer for the Milwaukee Brewers, the camera loved him and he had great comedic timing. I called up Lynn the next day and told him to bring Bob in to read. Bob might have never read a script before, but he fit the part perfectly.

With our cast set, we shot the pilot, which got picked up for a seven-episode opening season. For the next six years, I would be locked in a perpetual cockfight with ABC to keep the show on the air.

Here's how the finances of the television business worked from a studio's perspective. The magic number for syndication was eighty-eight. Once you made that many episodes, you were in the green in a major way. Syndicated shows mean reruns, and reruns mean money in the studio's pocket far after a show's inevitable cancellation. With twenty-two episodes in a season, I needed to keep a show on the air for four seasons before hitting the jackpot. This is all to say that I was looking for longevity and sustainability in a television series. *Mr. Belvedere* checked all the boxes. You could do anything with that effete butler—seat him beside the drunk uncle at Thanksgiving, commission him to get tickets to a baseball game, have him fix a leaky faucet.

Now that the show is a distant memory, I'll admit that it was a bit. . . wonky. Let's put it this way: it wasn't going to win any Emmys. But *Mr. Belvedere* was the little show that could. ABC hated it, tossing it into a number of brutal time slots, but it continually beat the competition and earned a second season order. However, ABC got a new president when *Belvedere* faced its third season. Lou Ehrlich was a good friend, but he hated—and I mean hated—the whole song and dance of Mr. Lynn Aloysius Belvedere.

"Say goodbye to your precious butler," he told me over the phone.

"Television isn't for Ivy League snobs like you—it's for middle America. Killing that butler will be the biggest mistake of your career."

But a few weeks later, I got wind from an inside source that ABC was holding a meeting to decide whether *Mr. Belvedere* had drunk his last martini. My source told me it wasn't looking good. I called my research department and told them to get ready for war.

"I want you to run every diagnostic on the show's performance. Then slant it more dramatically than the Tower of Pisa."

By the end of the day, I had a thick packet of semi-faulty data that argued for the sanctity of *Mr. Belvedere*.

"Print twenty copies," I told my research department. "And remove the Fox watermark."

That night, my executive Ed Gradinger and I executed a midnight raid on ABC. We played hearts in my office until ten o'clock, when we drove to the network offices. When the guard asked for our names, I slipped a hundred-dollar bill into his hand. Ten minutes later, Ed and I were planting our anonymous research in ABC's boardroom. We left a packet for every chair and sneaked away in the shadows.

The following day, Lou Ehrlich and his team entered their power meeting to indisputable data backing *Mr. Belvedere*. Lou called me before lunch to confirm we were back on the water.

"The numbers don't lie," I told him.

That didn't mark the end of my efforts to keep the show alive. By the next season, the eloquent Brandon Stoddard had replaced Lou Ehrlich as president of ABC. Stoddard was a stuck-up scholar from the East Coast who wouldn't be caught dead without a bow tie and a three-piece suit. To put it simply, he wasn't the target demographic of *Mr. Belvedere*.

"This show is a piece of shit," Stoddard told me over lunch.

"It's charming!" I responded.

"In last week's episode, the kid faked the death of his hamster, Inky, to get a dog."

"Well, it's lucrative."

"I'm canning the show. I don't care about what tricks you pulled on my predecessors, but your butler no longer fits the brand of ABC."

Understand this: with three seasons shot, I was up to sixty-six episodes. A fourth season renewal would put me into syndication play. I grabbed Stoddard's ankle and wouldn't let go—*Belvedere* wasn't going down in the eleventh hour. After hours of arguing across a white tablecloth, Stoddard begrudgingly agreed to ordering a thirteen-episode season—not the twenty-two that I would need to hit the magic number of eighty-eight episodes.

"Fine," I told him as we paid the bill. "But when you pick up the back nine episodes midseason, I get a bonus."

"Whatever you say. It's not going to happen."

A few months later, *Belvedere* had swept its audience, and Brandon Stoddard added nine more episodes to its fourth season.

You couldn't kill *Mr. Belvedere* with a stick. It ran for six seasons and received zero awards—save for an Emmy for Outstanding Lighting. However, it did rake in over $60 million in profits. I suppose if you endorse something enough times, the people around you will start to believe in your product.

A quitter never wins, and a winner never quits.

In the entertainment industry, hard lines in the sand are virtually nonexistent. You can always leverage a different outcome in a business transaction. A sense of respectful defiance in the face of rejection doesn't work every time, but you're bound to squeak out a few wins if you stick to your guns until the bitter end. Lou Ehrlich and Brandon Stoddard telling me that *Mr. Belvedere* was dead didn't mean the show was getting canceled. Rather, it meant that I hadn't done enough to get the show renewed. . . *yet*. That's the main question you have to ask yourself while selling in this business: Have I done enough yet? And if I haven't, what course of action can I take to reach my goal?

Save objectivity for the doctors and lawyers. When you're selling television shows, you can always swing the table in your favor.

Just as my division was starting to shape up, the finances of Fox came crashing down. Alan Hirschfield couldn't catch a break, with box office flops ranging from *Six Pack* to *Rhinestone*. Marvin Davis's tendency to hurl cash at every street corner didn't help the studio's souring finances. Ultimately, the owner decided to find a studio chief with more panache. Barry Diller was the clear candidate. As the president of Paramount, Barry had taken the industry by storm with films like *Raiders of the Lost Ark* and *Trading Places*. I'd last spoken with Barry when I turned down his offer to license *Gone with the Wind* to ABC. In response, he'd said something to the tune of, "I'll get you back if it's the last thing I do." Now that I was his employee, I figured he would take pleasure in serving me with a severance package.

I remember making the long trudge from my office to the administrative building where Barry was settling in. It was good while it lasted, I thought to myself. My final walk through the lot.

I gave his door a few raps and popped my head in.

"Congratulations, Barry," I said. "I suppose I'm destined for Siberia." He glanced at me for a millisecond and returned to his boxes.

"As long as you maintain your numbers, you can keep your job."

I couldn't believe it. But that was how Barry ran the studio. He was all about the quality of the operation; he took egos out of the equation.

With Barry Diller at the helm, the boys' club of Fox was gone, never to return. He kept his office at a chilly sixty-five degrees. On one of our Tuesday morning meetings, a senior executive showed up wearing a ski jumpsuit with padded gloves.

"You're not funny," Barry grumbled.

"But I'm warm."

Rather than encouraging Marvin Davis's culture of excess, Barry operated under the philosophy that change only comes through long hours of work. While others believed in working smarter, not harder, Barry liked to work smarter *and* harder. To put it simply, he scared everyone shitless. During a dinner at the Ivy, he made the network head Garth Ancier faint in the bathroom. Jonathan Dolgen commented that Barry Diller's number was 213-PAIN. Before stepping into his office, you'd better have something to say and an ability to defend it—otherwise Barry would cut your balls off and hang them on his mantel.

No matter how early I pulled into the Fox garage or how late I left the office, Barry's Jaguar convertible was always parked adjacent to my spot. It scared the whole lot; people thought that Barry never slept. It took me over a year to crack Barry's trick. While Barry was traveling in New York, I noticed his Jaguar in its regular spot.

"When was the last time you drove that convertible?" I asked him when he returned.

"The first day of my contract with Fox. It creates a mystique, doesn't it?"

As it turned out, Barry had three cars at home that he toggled through. The Jaguar was his decoy, planted to inspire fear within his underlings.

There was one moment when I saw a glimmer of humanity in Barry. To perfect my golf stroke, I had joined the Brentwood Country Club, where Barry's father was also a member. Mr. Diller demanded that management maintain its pool at a toasty eighty-five degrees, which cost the club thousands of dollars. When the board asked if I could inspire any mercy on behalf of Mr. Diller, I told Barry the whole story. He reclined in his chair, making spiders with his fingers.

"My father has a pool at home that he keeps at eighty-five degrees—he's doing this to be malicious. Now you know my backstory."

Even bosses fear their fathers.

I suppose some of the toughest suits in town still have a father complex. Though I couldn't imagine Barry backing away from a fight, he wasn't about to tangle with his old man. I told the board I couldn't move the needle, and Mr. Diller kept swimming in the club's steaming pool without interruption.

When you've been at the wrong end of your boss's tirades for a while, it can be refreshing to remember that everyone has a soft spot. It might not be readily visible, but it's there somewhere.

Despite Barry's militant crackdown, each year Marvin Davis hosted the Carousel Ball, a diabetes fundraiser that attracted every glamorous figure in the business. The event reflected Marvin to the tee—it couldn't have been more over-the-top. Meanwhile, I had just gotten a series on the air called *Cover Up* starring Jon-Erik Hexum, a young star whom I deemed the next Clark Gable. The show was a hit and destined for multiple seasons of programming. While I was flying to Denver for Marvin's ball, my assistant called me on the air phone.

"Hexum's dead!" she cried.

Hexum, who needless to say was not a Rhodes scholar, had decided to entertain himself with a gun between scenes. Apparently his idea of fun was playing Russian roulette with blanks. If you aren't aware, take this as a free public warning: blanks can be lethal at close range. When Hexum slipped a gun into his mouth and pulled the trigger, the blast lodged a piece of skull into his brain and caused severe hemorrhaging. Within a few hours, he was dead.

I had never been so angry—largely because the whole affair was so stupid and avoidable. When Marvin greeted me in Denver, I could barely speak.

"Lighten up, square deal," he barked. "We'll cast a new lead—it'll be fine. You're ruining my party with your negative energy."

I nearly slapped my boss across the face. Our star was dead. Not only was Hexum a nice kid who shouldn't have died, I knew the show wouldn't rebound after losing its main character. I had a few less-than-polite words for Marvin before I turned on my heel and boarded the Fox jet. The pilot took me straight back to Beverly Hills, where I spent the afternoon on the phone with casting directors, searching for someone to replace Hexum.

Meanwhile in Denver, Marvin was incensed for my public display of defiance. I had ruined his party by pouting, and he was prepared to fire me. I managed to dodge him for a few weeks, but I could sense my impending demise. I told my assistant Barbara to check the status of Marvin's jet every morning. I knew that Marvin didn't have any real reason to be in Los Angeles; an incoming flight meant I could start packing my things. In the meanwhile, I did my best to forget about my feud with my billionaire employer.

I remember Barbara peeking her head into my office like a mole, her eyes like saucers.

"When does he land?" I asked.

"Around noon," she said and took a seat at her desk.

I considered visiting the set of one of my shows or feigning a cold, but our beef had gone on far too long. I sure as hell wasn't going to apologize, which meant I had to face the wrath of Marvin Davis.

I was sitting in my office with the door closed when Marvin entered the building. I waited for Barbara to open the door with Marvin on her heels, but her knock never came. Over an hour later, I looked into the hallway and found Marvin stepping out of Barry Diller's office.

"Let's get dinner," Marvin boomed. An hour later, we were sitting at a restaurant with a stockpile of fancy food.

"We need to clear the air," he mumbled, jamming a fistful of almonds into his mouth.

"I'm a television exec," I said. "I care about my shows, and I care about my cast. That takes precedent over my party manners."

"Don't act like this business isn't about appearances," Marvin said. "We all play the game."

"Marvin—I'm not going to beg for my job. My numbers speak for themselves." *Here it comes*, I thought to myself.

"Your numbers aren't all you have. You should thank Barry Diller." With that, Marvin rose and reached his massive hand across my table with a smile. Just like that, we buried the hatchet. It became expressly clear that if you're in a knife fight in an alley, you want Barry Diller at your back.

Not everyone is replaceable.

To my profound disappointment, *Cover Up* was fated for cancellation the moment poor Hexum pulled his trigger. Hollywood has a surplus of available actors, but Hexum was the lifeblood of the show. Not only did he have movie-star looks, the kid could act better than any backup option.

At the risk of sounding vain, I believe that my own irreplaceability motivated Barry to protect me from Marvin Davis. God knows I did enough to get canned after my episode at the Carousel Ball. But while Barry Diller's steely approach to business didn't match my demeanor, he knew that qualified studio heads with tested track records were in short supply. Just as Hexum made *Cover Up* work, I was the locomotive for my division.

My little spat with Marvin came at the ideal time. Though Marvin and Barry's relationship started out with love, it had taken a dramatic turn toward hate. Marvin missed the good old days when he and Alan Hirschfield gorged themselves at fancy restaurants and caroused around the city. Barry wasn't interested in any of that. In fact, he was gumming over a burning resentment toward Fox's owner. Throughout Marvin's campaign to recruit Barry to the studio, he failed to mention that the studio was $600 million in debt. The banks refused to extend any more credit, and Marvin reneged on his promise to pump $100 million of his own money into the studio. Barry, the whiz kid of entertainment who had just broken ties at Paramount, found himself at the helm of a sinking ship.

Though Marvin hardly batted an eye at Barry's threats to sue him for fraud, it must have been weighing on him. He came up with the idea of selling Marc Rich's original share of Fox to Rupert Murdoch.

"If you sell that share to Rupert," Alan Hirschfield told Marvin in confidence, "he'll make out with the entire company." But Marvin waved him off.

"I can handle Murdoch," Marvin said. Rupert signed on the dotted line, birthing Hollywood's most ill-fitting partnership. While Marvin was a bull in a china shop, Rupert was quiet, deliberate, and all about business. Marvin would find that the only man less fun than Barry Diller was Rupert Murdoch. The Australian-American prodigy hadn't risen to the pinnacle of the media business out of happenstance. As the dauphin of News Corp., he knew how to navigate a massive corporation. That meant no more wasteful spending and no more spectacle.

The fork in the road came in the form of Metromedia, which owned six television stations. Rupert and Barry believed that acquiring the company would give them a shot of joining the distribution business. ABC, NBC, and CBS were the only networks at the time, but the new powers at Fox believed they could launch a fourth. Metromedia would ultimately form the nucleus of the Fox Broadcasting Company (FBC), a major network in today's market. This type of aggressive chatter was far over the head of Marvin Davis. For him, Fox was a trophy to display—not a cutting-edge company to transform the industry climate.

When the Metromedia chairman John Kluge agreed to sell the company for $2 billion, Marvin insisted that the figure was far too high. But Rupert and Barry were incredulous and backed Marvin into a corner. I never saw Marvin's bank statement, but I have reason to believe that his finances were overleveraged. He didn't have $1 billion lying around, and he had run out of Fox assets to sell.

After months of indecision, Marvin sold his Fox stake to Rupert for $575 million. He managed to retain Pebble Beach, which Rupert viewed as worthless window dressing. Soon enough, Marvin got $841 million for Pebble Beach—over $100 million more than Fox's initial price—from the Japanese businessman Minoru Isutani. Isutani had plans to replace the golf course with condos, but Marvin knew very well that his vision would never be realized. The California Coastal Commission prohibited housing developments that close to the scenic coastline.

"My way of getting back at the Japanese for Pearl Harbor," Marvin told me when Isutani had to eat his investment.

But as far as entertainment was concerned, the gargantuan oilman had relinquished his power. Alan Hirschfield was right: Marvin Davis couldn't keep up with Rupert Murdoch.

In the end, business beats pleasure.

Hollywood might be known as an industry of excess, but at its core it's a nuts-and-bolts business that requires intelligence and savvy. While the best moguls might seem like they're living carefree lives befitted with champagne flutes and Cadillacs, it takes an elite business IQ to keep a high post in Hollywood. Marvin Davis had the lifestyle down, but he didn't have the industry grind that drove Rupert Murdoch to the top of the game. If you're drawn to Hollywood for the perks instead of the work, you're here for the wrong reason.

I first met Rupert Murdoch in Barry Diller's boardroom. Everyone present was walking on eggshells. The media had primed Rupert as an entrepreneurial genius and a business Jedi. And with his background in newspapers, none of us had a rapport with him.

If I hadn't seen ten thousand pictures of Rupert, I wouldn't have guessed that he'd amassed a multibillion-dollar empire. Rupert sat in the back of the boardroom, completely silent as our finance executives milled through the state of the company. I remember the brown slits of his eyes flickering and a yellow legal pad squared before him. He took concise notes in a relaxed shorthand. When it was time for Rupert to listen, he listened. When it was time for him to speak, he asked all the right questions in a concise, probing manner. Rupert wasn't one to delegate; he demanded 100 percent comprehension of his company's undertakings.

Rupert cut the meeting short when he noted he was flying out of Los Angeles that afternoon.

"I booked the Fox jet," I said.

"We have a jet?" Rupert asked.

"Yes, we do." Rupert looked baffled.

"I usually fly coach. May I join you?"

"Of course," I replied. "May I join *you*?"

Among Lew Wasserman, Mark Goodson, Kirk Kerkorian, Marvin Davis, and Barry Diller, I had endured my fair share of titans. Rupert Murdoch's brains outmatched the others by a landslide. His ability to hatch the Fox Broadcasting Company changed the landscape of the television business altogether. In the early days of Rupert's network, the NBC president Brandon Tartikoff claimed that you needed to hook a coat hanger onto your TV set to gain access to FBC channels. Though the network started out as a distant fourth in relation to the others, Rupert fanned it into a roaring powerhouse. I had a front-row seat.

How I Paid My Mortgage
1986–1994

By the mid-1980s, Steven Bochco had risen to become one of the town's top television producers, responsible for writing and executive producing hits like *Hill Street Blues* and *McMillan & Wife*. Though Bochco had an overall deal with Mary Tyler Moore's production company, MTM, I hatched a plan to steal him. The key was Frank Rohner, the former head of CBS business affairs, whom I had befriended during my years at Goodson Todman. Frank had since left CBS, opened up his own law firm, and signed Steven Bochco. I took him out for lunch, during which I broached the prospect of poaching Bochco.

"That's a big ask," Frank said. "Everyone wants Bochco."

"Do I need to remind you of the Waldorf Astoria?"

During the Goodson Todman era, Frank and I visited New York City on business. Frank had brought his wife, who accused him of cheating. In a fit of rage, she threw the charm bracelet Frank had bought her from the top floor of the Waldorf Astoria Hotel. With the trinket costing Frank $10,000, he and I scaled the roof of the neighboring church and spent an hour searching for that bracelet. The whole charade ruined my suit. I figured Frank owed me, considering I ended up finding the damn thing. Now seemed as good a time as any to cash in the favor.

After a stellar meeting with Bochco, Frank and I agreed to a three-year deal that guaranteed Bochco $5 million, plus royalties and producing fees. Barry Diller had a conniption.

"You can't do that," he yelled.

"Sure I can. I have a discretionary fund that I can finance the deal out of."

"If Bochco goes over budget, you can count on tendering your resignation."

Barry had a point; Bochco had a proclivity to overshoot his budget. I needed to ensure that my new toy didn't break our bank. The first show that Bochco produced under the Fox banner was called *L.A. Law*. When I read the first pages and heard the series arc, I knew we had an instant hit on our hands. Bochco was smart enough to understand that he needed creative bodies with whom he could partner.

"I need a lawyer who can write steamy romance," he told me.

"I know the gal," I responded. Her name was Terry Louise Fisher—she had been a young lawyer in MGM's business affairs department who retired after writing a number of romance novels featured in drugstores. She went on to soar in the writers' room of the CBS police procedural *Cagney & Lacey*. Terry and Bochco hit it off, and they shared a creator credit. But Terry wasn't enough; Bochco wanted more legally minded scribes in his room.

"We found the only attorney who can write," I told him. "You're searching for a unicorn."

I was wrong. One morning, my assistant Barbara told me that she had received an unsolicited spec script from a junior litigator on the East Coast. She must have been bored that week because she didn't toss it in the waste bin, as was the fate of all other strangers' submissions. Instead, she read it.

"It's fantastic," she told me. "We should send it to Bochco."

The writer was the Boston attorney David E. Kelley, who has thirteen Emmys on his shelf and as strong a writing career as you can acquire in the television world. Bochco flew David out to Los Angeles and immediately offered him a position in the writers' room. David never returned to his law firm in Boston. When Bochco and Terry Louise Fisher locked horns on the direction of the series, David got promoted to executive producer.

He went on to write for *Doogie Howser, M.D.* and *Picket Fences*—both of which were major profit centers for the studio.

Listen to your assistant.

If you're using the person outside your office to man the phone lines and schedule meetings, you're not taking full advantage of your resources. Most assistants in entertainment are eager to slip the shadow of their bosses and make their mark on the business. That means scouting the city for fresh talent, reading every script under the sun, and networking like crazy. The raw hunger of young Hollywood presents a massive resource to industry bosses. By treating my assistant like a protégée instead of a secretary, I was able to sign one of the best writing talents to Fox. While Steven Bochco was the brain trust behind *L.A. Law*, David E. Kelley was the mind that kept the show running for eight seasons. The accolade of discovering him rests on Barbara's shoulders—not mine.

I pushed *L.A. Law* into production, holding my breath and praying that Bochco wouldn't exhaust our budget and get me into trouble with Barry Diller. My consolation was that dramas translate internationally, which meant I could sell foreign rights for roughly $200,000 per episode. Not something to rely on, but it provided a small cushion for spending surpluses. But by the time that Bochco delivered the final cut of the pilot, he was more than $250,000 over budget, and we had twenty-two more episodes to shoot. I stormed into Bochco's office in the Old Writers Building on the Fox lot.

"Steven—I gambled my career on you. You better rein it in," I said.

Bochco swore to me that we'd be on budget by the end of the series, and production forged ahead without interruption. By the end of the first season, we were $100,000 under budget, and Barry couldn't pick a bone with me. *L.A. Law* went on to win five Golden Globes and fifteen Emmys, including Outstanding Drama Series in 1987, 1989, 1990, and 1991. Not only did Bochco and Kelley generate hundreds of millions of dollars, they created a crown jewel for Twentieth Century Fox Television.

By the time that Bochco's term with Fox was up, the studio had made over $100 million on *L.A. Law*, and it wasn't showing any signs of slowing down. I had a long list of producers with offices on the lot, but Bochco was my anchor, along with Glen Larson. He was in the crosshairs of all my competitors, but I knew I had to keep him at Fox. Such would set the stage for the best deal of my career.

It started when Frank Rohner tipped me off to a deal that was brewing between Bochco and ABC.

"The entire town is going to pounce on this," Frank said. "With all you've done, I figured I'd give you a day's head start."

Now, this arrangement was between the creative, Steven Bochco, and the network, ABC. As a representative of the studio, I needed to insert Fox in a way that made financial sense to all parties. Here's what we settled on. Bochco would generate ten television series exclusive to ABC. If the network decided to move forward with a given series, it would cover the deficit financing for the first sixty-six episodes. Fox was on the hook to finance episodes sixty-seven and on. Remember: we needed to hit the magic number of eighty-eight before unlocking syndication money.

Now, if ABC decided that it didn't like Bochco's concepts for a series, it could pass with a penalty fee of $250,000 that went directly to Fox. If worse came to worst and the network passed on all ten series, we would recoup $2.5 million in penalty fees. So the question was as follows: How much should I offer Bochco to stay at Fox? I knew that my competitors were negotiating with ABC business affairs and crunching numbers internally. I had a figure in my mind, and it certainly exceeded my $5 million discretionary fund. I needed approval from Rupert Murdoch and Barry Diller.

The three of us met in Rupert's office, where I painted the picture for my bosses.

"I want to offer Bochco a straight fee of $50 million."

"I buy companies for $50 million," Rupert said.

"You are buying a company. Steven Bochco Productions."

They both had good reason for shock; the figure was unprecedented for a television producer—$50 million in 1990 inflates to over $90 million in 2016.

"Tell me why it makes financial sense to do this," Rupert demanded.

"If we have ten straight stinkers, we'll recoup $2.5 million, which would put us $47.5 million in the lurch. Out of that, we'd have foreign rights to Bochco's content, which means we could recoup $3 million per episode by selling to overseas markets. But that's all a moot point. None of that's going to matter."

"Why not?" Rupert asked.

"Because all it takes is one out of ten concepts to hit, and the studio will make a killing. Those are good odds with Steven Bochco at the helm."

That was enough for Barry and Rupert. We took out a life insurance policy on Steven Bochco and wrote a check for $50 million. As was expected after closing a groundbreaking deal, I received an onslaught of calls from the top executives of the era. Michael Eisner, the CEO of Disney, publicly stated that it was "the worst deal in the history of television." I knew that $50 million was a lot of money, but I wasn't insecure enough to let on any trepidation.

If there's talent, you pay.

What's Hollywood without talent? It's important to remember that people on the transactional side of the business—financiers, executives, producers, lawyers, and agents—are only employed insofar as creatives keep dreaming up wonky ideas. In consideration of Bochco's creative potential, he easily deserved every cent of his $50 million check.

The trick for a studio head, of course, is separating the real talent from the noise. In a town saturated with wannabe writers who believe they're better than the pros, you have to be careful that you're betting on the right horse when you're making a colossal deal like the one I made with Bochco. That was perhaps the most important part of my role at Fox: finding which creatives deserved a max deal. Choosing Steven Bochco wasn't a mistake.

Though I had gotten approvals from the powers of Fox and inked the paperwork, I had to make a final consummate sacrifice to keep Bochco happy. For the past three years, he had been holding offices in a dumpy corner of the lot. He demanded an upgrade, and we didn't have anywhere to put him.

Meanwhile, I was running a miniature fiefdom out of the television building, equipped with a basketball court, pool tables, and pinball machines. Half the time, I could stroll into the office wearing a polo shirt and loafers. Perhaps my aggressive offer sent Barry's radar blaring, because he caught my arm shortly after signing the Bochco deal.

"Where do you keep your office?" he asked.

"In a galaxy far, far away," I replied. I didn't want Barry Diller popping in whenever he saw fit. But that he did, and when he saw the carnival that I'd set up, he nearly blew a gasket.

"Say goodbye to your playground," he said. "You're moving to the executive building." That was the end of my weekday polo routine; rubbing elbows with Barry meant wearing a suit every day.

I knew I was being forced to abandon my offices, but Bochco didn't know that. So I called him up and offered him the television building.

"You'd do that for me?" Bochco exclaimed.

"Anything to keep you happy," I said.

With a $50 million bank deposit and a shiny new office, Bochco got to work on his ten series for ABC. He called the first one *NYPD Blue*, which ran for twelve seasons and made north of $250 million for the studio.

If I learned anything from the studio's biggest hits, it's that arrogance is kryptonite. For example, after season one of *L.A. Law*, the TV star Harry Hamlin made a series of ridiculous demands. I called a meeting with Bochco, Harry, and his agent in an effort to find a middle ground. But Harry and his agent wouldn't budge.

"We need a development fund, a guarantee to direct two episodes of the next season, and $75,000 per episode," the agent said.

"That's it?" I asked.

"Yep."

"Okay, no. Thanks for the first season, Harry." Harry turned white as a ghost. His agent saw his client's loyalty waning at an astronomical rate.

"You're gonna cut your star actor that easily?"

"Steven—are you prepared to lose him?" I asked. Steven started laughing.

"With those terms? Yeah." And just like that, Harry was off the show. He allowed his ego to persuade him that he was indispensable.

Years later on *NYPD Blue*, Bochco was smitten by the industry's top cinematographer, who demanded $10,000 per episode. Our backup choice was comparatively skilled and half the price.

"Why don't we all sleep on it?" I suggested. When Bochco came into my office the next day, he had made up his mind.

"Our first choice is worth the extra money. Let's get him."

"You didn't hear?!" I asked. "He got decapitated in a car accident last night. We have no choice but to go with the second guy."

Of course, the cinematographer was perfectly fine, save for his rate being too high. We hired the second cinematographer, who did a great job, and my white lie prevented war with Bochco. The point is that everyone who experiences success tries to overreach. Even Bochco fell subject to the spell of arrogance. At his peak, I remember him prodding at Glen Larson's string of misses.

"It's simple," he'd say. "Glen lost his fastball."

But Bochco, like the best producers, was fated to have one big miss: *Cop Rock*, a police drama that masqueraded as a Broadway musical. The show's cast of cops would be booking a bad guy and then randomly burst into song. It made *Manimal* look like *Breaking Bad*.

"You must have altitude sickness," I told Bochco when he pitched it to me on the ski lift in Aspen. I didn't have a say in the matter—with Bochco's new deal with ABC, he had full license to move ahead. Big surprise, we got canceled after eleven episodes. *Cop Rock*'s only accolade was making it to number eight on *TV Guide*'s "50 Worst Shows of All Time."

Even stars strike out.

If you flip through the filmography of entertainment's greatest creators, you can't help but scratch your head over a few horrible titles. As frustrating as it is to watch a project go down in flames, everyone is entitled to a few bombs. It's akin to finance—you're not betting on every title to smash; you're betting on a *single* title to smash. So long as a creator has the chance to make a ringer, expect to put up with at least a few misses.

Regardless of the train wreck that was *Cop Rock*, Bochco's deal was the most lucrative in the history of Fox Television. In fact, it inspired Michael Eisner and Jeffrey Katzenberg, then the chairman of Disney, to approach me with an offer to run their television division. But operations at Fox were going smoothly, and I couldn't stop thinking about how much I hated my commute when I worked at Bennett Katleman Productions. Disney was even farther down the 101 freeway.

"I'm flattered," I told Eisner and Katzenberg. "But you guys are geographically undesirable."

Another tempting job offer came in the form of Cannon Films, an independent financier led by the Israeli producers Menahem Golan and Yoram Globus. They had big aspirations and an even bigger bank, and they needed a veteran of the business to run operations.

I remember sitting in their conference room, which they had catered with heaping buckets of fried chicken. As they wiped the poultry grease from their fingers, they offered me three times what I was making as president of Fox Television. The money was enough to make any guy perk his ears. But as I thought it over, it occurred to me that I'd rather work at Fox than have my conference room riddled with chicken bones. It turned out to be the right decision: Golan and Globus folded within a couple years.

⚙

With Glen Larson and Steven Bochco under Fox contracts and actively developing new shows, I turned my attentions to the next great producer of the time: James Brooks. In addition to countless television and feature projects, Brooks had directed and produced the Academy Award–winning Drama *Terms of Endearment*. Barry Diller had signed him for features, and I salivated at the prospect of recruiting him to television. One evening, I took him out to dinner with the intent of turning him to the dark side.

"I'm done screwing around with television," he said. "Only interested in movies moving forward."

By chance, I had just picked up a $50 million check for Glen Larson's first round of profits on *The Fall Guy*. I smacked the slip of paper on the dinner table and watched Jim's pupils dilate.

"Christ—I didn't make that much on *Terms of Endearment*, and I won the fucking Oscar!" he said.

It was Lew Wasserman's persuasion formula executed to a tee; inspire malcontent within the talent and offer a clear path to wealth. Within the next few months, Jim was developing *The Tracey Ullman Show* with us. A distant cousin to *Saturday Night Live*, the show was a thirty-minute sketch comedy show. It's remembered for launching Jim's next creation: *The Simpsons*. Though Jim had never done animation, his variety show gave him the opportunity to dabble with cheaply produced cartoons in short segments. When the first installment of *The Simpsons* broadcast on *The Tracey Ullman Show*, the world stopped what it was doing. That clump of yellow knuckleheads fumbling about Springfield enraptured people like I had never seen. After several installments, Jim and I discussed launching Homer's world into its own series. We went off and shot seven one-minute episodes spliced together to make a presentation film—all for the modest price of $1 million. For the sake of cost efficacy, we had the animation done in South Korea.

We tested our presentation of *The Simpsons* at a preview house in Los Angeles. These special screenings still endure in the film and television business. Random audiences are tasked to turn a dial based on enjoyment level as they watch a piece of programming. *The Simpsons* earned a score of ninety-eight. Thinking it must be a fluke, I held another screening to a fresh market in Las Vegas. Ninety-eight once again.

I couldn't believe it. I had developed more programs than I could count—all of which aimed to move the needle within the hearts of viewers—and this was the strike? I guess the public has a penchant for sloppily drawn yellow cartoons with severe overbites.

I knew I had solid gold that would play well with audiences; now came the heavy lifting of selling the show. Ever since Rupert and Barry created the Fox Broadcasting Company (FBC), I had had a first-look deal with the new network. That meant I had a contractual obligation to give FBC an exclusive opportunity to buy my shows before marketing them to other buyers. That deal put me in a terrible position. With ABC, NBC, and CBS as the tried-and-true networks of the era, FBC was a distant fourth. From a studio's perspective, I wanted my shows on one of the three major networks. But I couldn't squirm my way out of FBC's grip.

Here's where it got tricky: let's say that after a long deliberation, FBC decided to pass on a pilot that I developed. Technically, I could try to sell the show at one of the competing networks. But if I succeeded and the show became a smash, the executives at FBC—my bosses—would look like idiots for passing. If I sold to FBC, my show was on the fourth network, and if I sold to another network, Barry would kill me. God forbid the potential of my shows failing on FBC. That would give Rupert and Barry the opportunity to blame me for the network's struggling performance.

Such are the dilemmas of a studio president in the midst of a growing company. On the *Simpsons* front, I knew that Barry would give a hard pass because he didn't have a whimsical bone in his body. I needed to create leverage for myself, and the only way to achieve that involved slipping the pilot to another buyer.

I went to the smartest network executive that I knew, someone with the foresight to understand the brilliance behind *The Simpsons*. That was Bob Iger, the current CEO of Disney, who was running ABC at the time. I scheduled a private screening for Bob and Bob only. As I'd hoped, he saw the magic of Homer, Marge, Bart, and Lisa and offered to buy a full series on the spot.

"I'd love to sell it to you," I responded. "But I have to take it to Barry Diller first."

Later that week, Barry Diller walked out of the screening with a grimace on his face.

"I don't get it," he said. "The last successful animated show was *The Flintstones*."

"Exactly—the market will eat this up."

"Why would adults watch a cartoon?" he asked.

"Why not?"

"I'm not buying it," he said.

"No sweat," I replied. "Fair warning: Bob Iger has already made an offer."

"You can't sell this thing to ABC," Barry said.

"My hands are tied." I shrugged. "We spent a million dollars making the pilot, and Fox has a deal with James Brooks. I have a fiduciary obligation to try to sell the show."

"You have a bunker mentality," Barry growled. But he bought thirteen episodes of *The Simpsons*, which cost a whopping $13 million.

"It better work," Barry said.

"If it doesn't work, you can always fire me," I responded.

"No, I'll keep you here and torture you."

The executives at FBC slotted the show in on Thanksgiving—they figured it would bomb and didn't want to waste valuable airtime. It was quite the handicap—let's just say I didn't have an appetite for turkey and cranberry sauce that year. But to everyone's surprise, *The Simpsons* rolled over the competition. In the weeks to follow, the ratings continued to break barriers. We were a smash.

After the end of its first season, I treated my staff to a fancy dinner in New York.

"Anywhere you want—I'll get us a reservation."

"Il Mulino!" someone cried out.

Il Mulino was New York's most high-profile dining spot in the city; it took months to get a reservation. I called the restaurant and got the owner on the line.

"I'd like to make a reservation for twelve this evening."

"You've got to be kidding," snorted the Italian on the other end of the line.

"Do you have a family?" I asked.

"Yeah. What are you gonna do—threaten to kill 'em?"

"God, no," I said. "Do they watch *The Simpsons*?"

"Of course."

I told him that I was responsible for putting the world's top comedy on the air and offered to give him signed merchandise if he could confirm a reservation.

That night, a very unhappy party of twelve was forced to wait at the bar as we took their table. Such was the power of *The Simpsons*.

By the following year, *The Tracey Ullman Show*'s sixty-second cartoon sketch had become Fox's most lucrative piece of entertainment. In it's thirtieth season as of 2019, the show has raked in billions for Fox.

When your shot comes, take it.

There isn't anything more intimidating than tying your name to a fledgling project. After all, my cardinal value as the president of Fox Television was my taste, and I was going all in on a cartoon for adults. But when you know you have something special, you need to have the guts to swing for the fence. If you play it safe, you might never run the risk of getting chewed out or fired, but you'll be destined to mediocrity.

For the most part, business went on as usual despite Rupert's growing media empire. I was responsible for making hit television shows and nothing else. That being said, there were select instances that roped me into News Corp.'s challenges. Rupert owned the largest, most lucrative news publication in the Far East: the *South China Morning Post*. Headquartered in Hong Kong, the paper was throwing off an annual excess of $60 million in profits. This was the period in which China was preparing to annex Hong Kong, and Rupert was concerned that the paper and its profits would be seized in such a case. I, along with seven other senior executives at Fox, was tasked to convince the Chinese to protect Rupert's profit center from looming political threats. Rupert gave me license to give away any piece of entertainment capital that they wanted.

"We need to hold on to that paper," he demanded.

Of course, I hadn't been briefed on any of this until two days before Barry Diller told me I was bound for Beijing. There was only one problem: my youngest son, Michael, was getting married the following day.

"You can record the wedding," Barry said.

I fought back and convinced Barry to push the trip back a day. After Michael's ceremony, I went straight to the airport and boarded a commercial flight to China, as the Fox jet didn't have permission to enter

Chinese airspace. I had a seat in business class, but once I flashed my identification at the gate, the flight attendants shuffled travelers around to give me a first-class seat. That was just the beginning of my royal welcome. When we arrived in Beijing, a stern Chinese man in a black suit tapped me on the shoulder.

"Mr. Katleman, I'm Mr. Chang. Please follow me."

Mr. Chang led me to a black limousine that was at my disposal for the length of my two-week trip. He was a member of the Chinese secret service.

"How about my luggage?" I asked.

"It's being transported to your room via helicopter, sir."

Mr. Chang promptly presented me with a two-week itinerary, which mapped my schedule down to the last minute with meetings and banquets. Off we went to the State Morning House, the opulent hotel where Queen Elizabeth II stayed during her trips to China. I called my assistant upon checking in to my suite, bemoaning the fact that I hadn't brought enough suits. Within ten seconds, I heard a knocking on the door. I answered to find a representative from the *South China Morning Post*.

"Don't worry, Mr. Katleman," he said with a perfect English accent. "We'll launder your shirts for you."

It dawned on me that the phones were tapped. I rushed over to the adjacent room, which housed Richard Searby, the chairman of News Corp. and Rupert's right-hand man. I put a finger to my lips when he answered his door, then I led him into the bathroom and turned on the shower.

"They bugged our rooms," I whispered.

"Jesus, are you sure?"

"Sure as death." Richard chewed this over for a moment.

"What are we doing in the bathroom?"

"I saw in a movie that they can't hear you with the shower on. I want to see if it works."

"You need to watch less movies and more news," Richard said.

So began a two-week binge of schmoozing in an effort to stabilize control over the *South China Morning Post*. As we got into the nitty-gritty, I adhered to my instructions and asked the minister of culture what Fox movies they might want to broadcast for the Chinese public.

"We're partners," I remember saying. "Whatever we have is welcome to you."

Of Fox's film arsenal, the Chinese were primarily interested in two titles: *Patton* and *The Sound of Music*.

"I'll tell you what," I told the minister of culture. "You have commercials when you telecast, right?"

"Of course," the minister replied.

"How many commercials an hour?"

"About ten."

"Why don't we hang on to two out of the ten commercials every hour—only for *Patton* and *The Sound of Music*. Let's call the movies and the rest of the advertising on me."

We had ourselves a deal. I immediately placed a call to Bobby Morin, who was in charge of syndication and advertising at the time.

"I need you to contact the head honchos of advertising at Pepsi-Cola and General Foods—they're massive brands in Asia. Tell them we have grade-A advertising time that we can sell pronto."

"What's the big deal?" Bobby asked.

"If the Chinese public lights up like the executives did when I mentioned *Patton* and *The Sound of Music*, five hundred million people are going to be tuning in to these commercials."

We ended up getting over $1 million from commercials for every run of *Patton* and *The Sound of Music*. With inflation, that's over $2 million in modern US dollars. More, our mission to make nice with the Chinese was a major success. News Corp. managed to hang on to the *South China Morning Post* until Rupert sold the paper to the real estate tycoon Robert Kuok in 1993.

I had survived quite a few monsters after ten years at the top of a television studio. The C-suite executive Lucie Salhany would be my next major obstacle. With FBC growing at lightning speed, Barry tapped her as chair of Twentieth Television. In other words, I had to answer to her. I suppose that my relationship with Lucie was fated to go down the tubes from the very onset. Shortly after she took the reins at Fox, the two of us grabbed dinner at the Ivy in West Hollywood.

I can't say anything for certain, but I had the sense that that Lucie was interested in starting a personal relationship to go along with our professional one. I, for one, wasn't interested crawling in bed with the new sheriff in town. Needless to say, the rest of the dinner and the ensuing months at the office were rather awkward. That didn't prevent Lucie from inviting me to game night on Saturdays, which was my personal version of hell. After I ducked Lucie a few too many times, she and I started to lock horns. Our first major standoff revolved around FBC's late-night show. Barry and Rupert had just canceled Joan Rivers's variety show, and Lucie got the idea to hire the comedian Chevy Chase. By this point in my career, I had been around the bush for quite some time, and I knew a bad idea when it hit me in the face.

"This is a horrific idea," I said to a room with Rupert, Barry, and Lucie. "You need a star for late-night programming, and Chevy isn't a star."

"He's a star on *SNL*!" Lucie fired back at me.

"He gets five minutes of screen time. Do what you will, but don't dip into my department's fund."

My popularity rating dipped within the company because I disagreed with a pretty woman. Fast-forward a few months later while I was in the Hamptons on business. Whom did I find at a restaurant, carousing with his posse? None other than Chevy Chase.

"You go on the air in a few weeks—shouldn't you be doing dry runs?" I asked.

"I can phone it in," replied Chevy.

Watching *The Chevy Chase Show* was like putting pins in your eyes. While Fox had promised that the show would rake in over five million viewers nightly, it pulled in a meager two million. Within four weeks, Fox cut its losses and pulled the plug. Rupert Murdoch approached me months later at a fund-raising dinner for Governor Pete Wilson.

"I lost over $50 million on Chevy Chase. You live and you learn."

I would never wish ill upon my own company, but nothing feels better than a good old-fashioned *I told you so*.

Despite my share of kerfuffles with Lucie, I still liked her as a person, at least for the time being. One day I heard her sniffling from her office, and when I entered she was sobbing into her hands.

"I have a lump on my breast, and they think it's cancer."

"I have a guy for that," I replied.

"This isn't show business. You can't place a call and make it all go away."

"Sure I can—I'm friends with Action Doc."

If you don't remember, Jerry "Action Doc" Steiner was a consistent loser in my poker game, along with Dan Tana. He had since become a renowned breast cancer surgeon out of Cedars-Sinai Hospital. Jerry worked his magic and saved Lucie's life. I'm not taking any credit for Jerry's medical expertise, but it would have been nice if Lucie cut me a little slack after displaying empathy in her darkest moment.

Years later, I had a great show called *Anything but Love* entering its fourth season on the air. The show was smart, cheap, and the critics' darling with a great cast of Jamie Lee Curtis and Richard Lewis. While vacationing in Positano, I got an urgent call from my assistant, who indicated that Lucie was canceling my show. The resort's towel boy had never heard the expletives that I amplified through the phone. We were on the cusp of syndication, which meant massive profits for my division, and Lucie lacked the courtesy to call me directly. It would have been one thing if the show was garbage, but everyone liked it. I booked a flight to Los Angeles that afternoon, intent on saving the show.

My first stop was Bob Iger, the standing chief of ABC, who would later become the CEO of a little company called Disney. If Lucie was going to work behind my back, I would work behind hers. After an elaborate sales pitch and hordes of research data, I managed to salvage the situation and secure a season-four pickup at ABC. Whatever anger I felt, multiply that by ten and give it to Lucie. Hell hath no wrath for a woman's scorn.

"You undermined my authority!" she screamed into my face.

"You canceled my show!" I shouted back.

My fix for the problem ended up being a temporary one. By the time I got the show re-renewed, all the good time slots were filled. *Anything but Love* went on at nine o'clock every Saturday night. It was like walking into the Vietnam War. The show failed to find an audience and dwindled to kindling. Chalk up one more point for Lucie Salhany, the dream killer.

Lucie's presence at Fox coincided with some major changes at the studio—most notably the departure of our fearless leader, Barry Diller. I started to smell that something was amiss while in Aspen with Rupert and Barry. As Rupert and I rode the gondola to the summit, he made a remark that really ruffled my feathers.

"You know, Harris, you make quite a bit of money."

"Fox Television is making over $250 million this year. I rest my case."

"I know all that. But the editor of the *London Times* doesn't make what you make. I just find it curious."

I skied down that run like I was chasing the Olympic slalom record. I found Barry sitting in the Tippler, the fancy watering hole at the base of the mountain.

"If I'm making too much money, you're making *way* too much money," I told him. But Barry was in Aspen mode. He wasn't his prickly self.

"Relax, Harris. We're doing fine."

Six months later, it was announced that Barry would be leaving the company. I can't say that I was completely shocked; with Rupert and Barry at the helm of the company, you had a rottweiler and a pit bull.

At the end of the day, Rupert had ownership of the company, and Barry wasn't willing to play second fiddle. In hindsight, leaving Fox was the best thing Barry could have done. He went on to become a billionaire through his managerial and investment roles at QVC, USA Network, and IAC.

With Barry gone, Lucie Salhany's power expanded, and my life got much more difficult. It had been forty-two years since I had been an office boy at MCA, and fourteen years since I transitioned to president of Twentieth Century Fox Television. I had outlasted three standing CEOs in Dennis Stanfill, Alan Hirschfield, and Barry Diller. I had endured the chaotic reign of Marvin Davis and the calculated dynasty of Rupert Murdoch. And most importantly, I had developed some of the most successful television shows in history. It was time to let someone else take the reins.

Know when to fold your cards.

It's no secret that no one runs a studio forever. I'm personally of the mind that it's best to leave on your own terms. Throughout my tenure at Fox, I always knew that I was working on borrowed time. While I imagine that job security feels good—I can't be entirely certain, as I've never experienced it before—the competitiveness of my role pushed me to strive for the absolute best. Stress is a part of every industry. Rather than letting the pressures of business bring you down, I find it healthier to confront them as motivation to do something special with your career. After all, there comes a point when you have to hang up your cleats. And when you do, you're going to ask yourself if you did your life's work justice. You don't want to hesitate when that question comes knocking around.

With two years left on my contract, I elected to segue into a production deal on the lot. I had made a handful of pilots—none of which got picked up to series—when I was approached to be the COO of none other than Mark Goodson Productions. Mark had bought out Bill's share of their company before passing away from pancreatic cancer, and his executors needed help handling Mark's hulking portfolio of shows. Mark had always told me that one day I would return to the game show business, and in the end he was right. I dissolved my fledgling production deal and returned to work under the banner of Mark Goodson.

Choose your executors carefully.

That is, of course, if you're lucky enough to have a legacy at the end of your life. In addition to myself, there were four men running Mark's estate: Jeremy Shamos, his former son-in-law; Marvin Goodson, his brother; and Richard Schneidman, a CPA. They were all well intentioned, but they were clueless when it came to handling the estate. They made a number of critical errors, the last of which ended in the company's sale. Mind you: Mark Goodson Productions owned *To Tell the Truth*, *The Price Is Right*, and *Family Feud*—all of which are running today. Talk about flowing cash. But the four main executors didn't foresee such long runs, and they wanted to line their pockets with a sale. They ended up accepting a price of $60 million. To put things into perspective, *The Price Is Right* alone has thrown off profits of over $400 million. Mark Goodson Productions was conservatively worth $500 million, but no one could see it. At the end of the day, money begets power, and power begets problems.

So what does retirement look like for a man who's devoted his entire life to entertainment? It may sound like recycled wisdom, but distance from the office has opened my eyes to the value of family. I'm lucky enough to have three children, seven grandchildren, and nine great-grandchildren. Both of my sons have made their careers in the industry; Steven is a successful entertainment attorney at Greenberg

Traurig, one of the world's eminent law firms, and Michael is a director/ executive producer involved in television shows like *The Last Ship, Zoo,* and most recently *The Fix* on ABC. My daughter, Lisa, is the glue that keeps us all together.

I'm afraid, however, that I haven't achieved stability with the women in my life. In addition to the countless moguls and creatives, I've survived five fleeting marriages. Luckily, I've exchanged olive branches with Carole, Marilyn, Irena, and Helen. Wife number five was a different story. I will not give her the dignity of referring to her by name—our "union" spanned thirty days of hell before the divorce settlement began. I can only say that I didn't do my due diligence. Luckily I found my current beau, Kathie Schlesinger. Crazy, kooky, and loyal to a fault, she's the one you want at your side to slay dragons with.

It's a tricky thing, reflecting upon your career. I've learned that life does not abide by the bell curve of a well-executed story. It's marked by failures, shortcomings, and episodes of extreme stress. But for me, all the trying moments were temporary. They always gave way to a tremendous adventure that I profoundly enjoyed. Just think: if I had listened to my father's advice, I would have dedicated my life to selling air-conditioning units at Sears. Instead, I ended up developing some of the most successful and influential shows of our time.

My days as a tastemaker may have come to a close, but I still live in the same house on the same hill that Kim Basinger convinced me to rollerblade down. There's something energizing about watching the relentless wheel of the entertainment industry from afar. I think about all the men and women working their tails off to bring creative ideas to the screen. I think about the actors, the writers, and the directors. I think about the producers of reality television, the financiers, and the agents. The sound mixers, the vitamin D–deprived workers toiling in the editing bays, unionized and non-unionized crews. They're all a part of the largest creative projects our society has to offer.

Life is a celebration.

Among all the others, this lesson from my mother takes the cake. Sixty-eight years have passed since I attended entertainment graduate school at MCA, and I still haven't gotten over the miracle that this industry even exists. It occurs to me there's one visceral drive that keeps the lights on. One consistent motivation that keeps the wallets of financiers open and the efforts of creatives active. An allegiance to stories.

After all, what's life but a collection of stories?

Acknowledgments (Harris Katleman)

This book wouldn't be complete without acknowledging the allies who helped me survive in Hollywood. I'd like to thank:

Lew Wasserman: My mentor who gave me the best education I could have hoped for.

Mark Goodson: A genius in television, but more importantly a true friend.

Edward Gradinger: The colleague who always had my back, even when it wasn't popular.

Gary Winnick: My dear friend who always has an opinion.

Bill Haber: My confidante who was always there and never wavered.

The network executives who had the good taste to buy my shows.

The verbal beatings that kept me from ever repeating a mistake.

My grandson and co-author Nick: Our family historian, who managed to capture my life on the page.

Last but not least, my dear friends who keep me laughing: David Baron, Tom Constance, Howard Curd, George Rosenthal, Marvin Chanin, Jeffery Rosenthal, Garry Briskman, Sandy Bresler, Mitch Blumenfeld, Rob Huizenga, Len my mysterious friend, and my poker pals and golf pals who never let me win.

Thank you for making my life so very special. Here's looking forward to ninety more years...

Acknowledgments (Nick Katleman)

I wouldn't have been able to co-write this book without my own mentors in Hollywood:

James Farrell: My first boss, who taught me what a full day of work looks like.

Rob Carlson: The man who taught me that good guys can win too.

Also, endless thanks to my family for their unconditional support:

Steve & Janet Katleman: The most loving parents I could ask for.

Sara & James Skahen: The happiest, most adventurous couple I know.

And of course, my grandfather Harris Katleman: The titan who never ceases to amaze.

Glossary

Nick Adams—American actor best known for starring in *The Rebel*, produced by Goodson Todman Productions. Passed away at the age of thirty-six from a prescription drug overdose.

Buddy Adler—Film producer at Columbia Pictures, who later became the production head of Twentieth Century Fox. Won the Academy Award for producing *From Here to Eternity*.

James T. Aubrey—Prodigious film and television executive known as "The Smiling Cobra." Served terms running ABC, CBS, and MGM throughout an illustrious career filled with countless scandals and successes.

Greg Bautzer—Dashing power attorney who represented clients including Kirk Kerkorian, James T. Aubrey, and Howard Hughes.

David Begelman—Two-faced film executive who held posts at MCA and the talent agency Creative Management Associates before heading Columbia Pictures. Ultimately committed suicide following a string of high-profile embezzlement scandals.

Harve Bennett—Prolific television producer responsible for the programs *Rich Man, Poor Man* and *The Six Million Dollar Man*. Later transitioned into film, producing the *Star Trek* movies.

Steven Bochco—Legendary television producer and writer, famous for creating series including *L.A. Law*, *NYPD Blue*, *Doogie Howser, M.D.*, and *Hill Street Blues*.

Richard Boone—American actor famous for his many roles in Westerns. Hosted *The Richard Boone Show*, produced by Goodson Todman Productions.

Marlon Brando—American icon and Academy Award–winning actor, best known for his roles in *On the Waterfront*, *The Godfather*, and *A Streetcar Named Desire*.

James L. Brooks—Television and film director, producer, and writer who swept the Academy Awards with *Terms of Endearment*. Transitioned to Fox Television, where he developed *The Tracey Ullman Show* and later *The Simpsons*.

Johnny Cash—Famous singer-songwriter, inducted into the Country Music, Rock and Roll, and Gospel Music Halls of Fame.

David Charnay—President and chairman of Four Star Productions.

Paddy Chayefsky—American playwright, screenwriter, and novelist who won three solo Academy Awards for Best Screenplay. Best known for *Marty*, *The Hospital*, and *Network*.

Moe Dalitz—Famed American gangster who earned his stripes bootlegging during Prohibition. Helped to shape the early casinos of Sin City, earning him the nickname "Mr. Las Vegas."

Bob Daly—Studio head who presided over CBS and Warner Bros. before becoming chairman and CEO of the Los Angeles Dodgers.

Marvin Davis—Larger-than-life oil mogul who purchased Twentieth Century Fox, Pebble Beach, the Beverly Hills Hotel, and the Aspen Skiing Company. Peak net worth of $5.8 billion.

Barry Diller—Tough-as-nails executive who served as vice president of development at ABC, chairman and CEO of the Paramount Picture Company, and chairman and CEO of Fox. Later became chairman of Expedia and IAC, a conglomerate that controls companies including Match.com, CollegeHumor, Tinder, and the *Daily Beast* among others. Peak net worth of $3.1 billion.

Jonathan Dolgen—Hot-tempered head of Fox's film financing department who ultimately became the co-chief of Paramount Pictures.

Michael Eisner—Studio chief who served as president and CEO of Paramount Pictures before becoming the chairman and CEO of the Walt Disney Company.

Don Fedderson—Television executive producer who created programs including *My Three Sons* and *Family Affair*.

Andrew J. Fenady—Television writer who penned *The Rebel, Branded,* and *The Man With Bogart's Face*.

Terry Louise Fisher—Former attorney who quit her practice to write the CBS procedural *Cagney & Lacey* and later the Fox drama *L.A. Law*.

Gerald Ford—Former US president who served from 1974 to 1977. Served as a member of the Fox board.

Clark Gable—Iconic American actor known as the King of Hollywood. Best known for starring in *Gone With the Wind*.

Jerry Giesler—Famous trial lawyer with a reputation for triumphing in "unwinnable" cases. Represented Charlie Chaplin, Bugsy Siegel, and Marilyn Monroe.

Bill Goetz—Studio executive who co-founded Twentieth Century Pictures, later named Twentieth Century Fox.

Jackie Gleason—Famous comedian known for his irreverent antics. Most famous for his work in *The Honeymooners* and *The Jackie Gleason Show*.

Mark Goodson—Co-founder of Goodson Todman Productions, the most dominant game show production company in the history of Hollywood. Peak net worth north of $450 million.

Peter Grad—Top television development executive at Fox who went on to become president of MTM Television.

Ed Gradinger—Head of business affairs at Columbia Pictures, who went on to become the President of New World Entertainment and MGM Television.

Cary Grant—Hollywood's classic leading man, known for starring in *Penny Serenade, None but the Lonely Heart*, and a number of Alfred Hitchcock films including *Suspicion* and *North by Northwest*.

Jerry Gross—President of Cinemation Studios who made a temporary living off exploitation films, known for their lurid content.

Bill Haber—Co-founder of the über-agency CAA.

Harry Hamlin—Successful television actor best known for his role in *L.A. Law*.

Alfred Hitchcock—One of the most influential directors and producers in film history, with classic films including *Psycho, Vertigo, North by Northwest*, and *The Birds*.

Alan Hirschfield—Studio executive who served as CEO of Columbia Pictures as well as chairman of Twentieth Century Fox.

Howard Hughes—Legendary business magnate whose interests ranged from the aviation industry to Hollywood. Produced hits including

Scarface before gaining control of the RKO film studio.

Bob Iger—Former president of ABC and standing CEO of Disney, who has leveraged the acquisitions of Pixar, Lucasfilm, Marvel, and most recently Twentieth Century Fox.

Beldon Katleman—Owner of the El Rancho Hotel and Casino in Las Vegas. Closely tied into the Jewish Mafia.

David E. Kelley—Attorney turned writer who became an executive producer on *L.A. Law*. Known for creating *Picket Fences*, *Chicago Hope*, and *Big Little Lies*.

Kirk Kerkorian—Armenian American media mogul who became president and CEO of the Tracinda Corporation. Owned the MGM film studio as well as the International Hotel, the MGM Grand Hotel, and the MGM Grand. Peak net worth of $16 billion.

Irvin Kershner—Acclaimed director of *The Rebel*, who moved into film with major franchise titles including *The Empire Strikes Back* and the James Bond film *Never Say Never Again*.

Adnan Khashoggi—Saudi Arabian mogul and international businessman who was implicated in the Iran-Contra affair as an arms dealer. A common fixture at Kirk Kerkorian's Las Vegas casinos.

Robert Kintner—Network executive who served as president of ABC and NBC. Left entertainment to serve as cabinet secretary for President Lyndon B. Johnson.

Sidney Korshak—Infamous lawyer and "fixer" for the Chicago outfit of the Mafia. Obtained major influence in Hollywood by befriending major titans of the business including Lew Wasserman, Robert Evans, and Kirk Kerkorian, among others.

Stanley Kramer—Acclaimed film director responsible for titles such as *It's a Mad, Mad, Mad, Mad World*; *High Noon*; and *The Defiant Ones*.

Jennings Lang—Senior agent at MCA whose affair with Joan Bennett led to being shot in the testicles.

Sherry Lansing—Former President of Twentieth Century Fox who went on to become the Chairman and CEO of Paramount Pictures. Served as the first woman to head a major film studio and earn a star on the Hollywood Walk of Fame in a producing capacity.

Glen A. Larson—Famed television producer and writer known for creating *Battlestar Galactica, Magnum, P.I., The Fall Guy*, and *Knight Rider*.

Barry Lowen—Senior development executive at MGM who followed me to Columbia and Fox.

George Lucas—Mastermind behind the *Star Wars* and *Indiana Jones* franchises and creator of Lucasfilm.

Fred MacMurray—Major American movie star best known for his role in *Double Indemnity* and the ABC television series *My Three Sons*.

Dean Martin—Nightclub singer turned actor best known as Jerry Lewis's counterpart in the Martin and Lewis comedy duo.

Les Moonves—Media titan who presided as president and CEO of Warner Bros. Television before becoming chairman of the board, president, and CEO of CBS Corporation.

Rupert Murdoch—Media magnate who has served as chairman and CEO of News Corporation and chairman and CEO of 21st Century Fox. Net worth of $17.8 billion.

Gary Newman—Chairman and CEO of the Fox Television Group. Responsible for shepherding programs like *Modern Family*, *The Americans*, *Empire*, and *American Horror Story*.

Clifford Odets—Elite playwright and screenwriter who served as the precursor to Arthur Miller, Paddy Chayefsky, Neil Simon, and David Mamet among others. Ran creative on *The Richard Boone Show* before his untimely passing.

Michael Ovitz—Co-founder and former chairman of über-agency CAA, who went on to become the president of the Walt Disney Company.

Bill Paley—Genius executive who expanded CBS from a fledgling radio company into the largest network in America.

Ronald Reagan—Actor turned president of the United States, who served from 1981 to 1989. Hosted *General Electric Theater*, the prominent competitor of the Goodson Todman–produced drama *The Rebel*.

Don Rickles—Pioneering comic and actor who popularized insult comedy.

Frank Rosenfelt—CEO of MGM under owner Kirk Kerkorian. Went on to become the chief executive of United Artists.

Rick Rosner—Television producer who rose to wealth with the MGM series *CHiPs*.

Elton Rule—President of ABC, who shepherded *The Don Rickles Show* among other landmark television programs.

Lucie Salhany—Chair of Twentieth Television, who became chair of FOX News network after Barry Diller's departure from the company. Left Fox to become CEO of United Paramount Network.

Benjamin "Bugsy" Siegel—Infamous American mobster who was one of the most feared gangsters of the early twentieth century. Served as a hitman before building the Flamingo, the oldest hotel on the Las Vegas Strip. Murdered in his girlfriend's home at the age of forty-seven.

Frank Sinatra—Musical legend and leader of the Rat Pack.

Dennis Stanfill—Former chairman of the board and CEO of Twentieth Century Fox.

Jimmy Stewart—Major American film icon known for starring in *It's a Wonderful Life*, *The Philadelphia Story*, and *Mr. Smith Goes to Washington*.

Brandon Tartikoff—Groundbreaking television executive who revitalized NBC with hits like *Hill Street Blues*, *L.A. Law*, *Law & Order*, *The Cosby Show*, and *Knight Rider*, among others.

Bill Todman—Co-founder and marketing genius behind Goodson Todman Productions, the most dominant game show production company in the history of Hollywood.

Jack Van Volkenberg—President of CBS Television.

Walter Wanger—Marquee studio executive and producer who served as president of the Academy of Motion Picture Arts and Sciences. Earned an Academy Award for producing *Cleopatra* after shooting talent agent Jennings Lang in the testicles.

Lew Wasserman—Legendary president of MCA who revolutionized the business by shifting power from the studio system to talent.

Sonny Werblin—President of MCA's television division, owner of the New York Jets, and chairman of Madison Square Garden. Created the modern ideal of the sports star by bringing marquee athletic events into the entertainment spotlight.

Nedrick Young—Academy Award–winning screenwriter known for penning *The Defiant Ones*.

Darryl F. Zanuck—Legendary studio executive who helped assemble the modern studio system. Started his career running production at Warner Bros. and ultimately co-founded Twentieth Century Pictures, which became Twentieth Century Fox.